Memes of Misinformation: Federal Spending

Unraveling the controversial, socio-economic and political issues behind those annoying social media memes

Julio C Castañeda Jr

Vernon Series in Communication

VERNON PRESS

www.vernonpress.com

In the Americas:
Vernon Press
1000 N West Street,
Suite 1200, Wilmington,
Delaware 19801
United States

In the rest of the world:
Vernon Press
C/Sancti Espiritu 17,
Malaga, 29006
Spain

Vernon Series in Communication

Library of Congress Control Number: 2017932061

ISBN: 978-1-62273-252-4

Table of Contents

Description

In this first installment of the Misinformation series, the author tackles complex socio-economic and political topics related to the economy of the United States, such as the federal budget, wasteful spending, the national debt, unemployment and social security. By breaking down each subject into layman's terms, the author clearly and concisely presents, in an unbiased manner, the facts behind the fake news, alternative facts, half-truths and general misinformation from the annoying headlines and memes cluttering social media on these volatile subjects.

Dedication

I would like to dedicate this book to my biggest fan and most awesome wife, Misty. Thanks for putting up with my particular brand of crazy. You make our journey so much more enjoyable.

Acknowledgements

Special thanks to those that have contributed by tediously proof-reading endless versions of this manuscript: Misty C, Maxi R, Karen P, Vince T, Val P and Sam T.

List of abbreviations

- AAA – Agricultural Adjustment Act
- ACA – Affordable Care Act
- AIG – American International Group
- ANOVA – Analysis of Variance
- BCE – Before Christ Event
- BLS – Bureau of Labor Statistics
- CBO – Congressional Budget Office
- CBP – US Customs & Border Protection
- CIA – Central Intelligence Agency
- CPI – Consumer Products Index
- CPS – Current Population Survey
- CWA – Civil Works Administration
- DC – Washington, District of Columbia
- DI – Disability Insurance
- DITF – Disability Insurance Trust Fund
- DJIA – Dow Jones Industrial Average
- DNDO – Domestic Nuclear Detection Office
- EB – Extended Benefits (for unemployment)
- ECB – European Central Bank
- EO – Executive Orders
- EU – European Union
- EUC – Emergency Unemployment Compensation
- FDIC – Federal Deposit Insurance Corporation
- FDR – Franklyn Delano Roosevelt, 32nd POTUS, also referred to as Franklyn Roosevelt, F.D. Roosevelt
- FEMA – Federal Emergency Management Agency
- FERA – Federal Emergency Relief Administration
- FHA – Federal Housing Administration
- FLETC – Federal Law Enforcement Training Center
- FLOTUS – First Lady of the United States
- FOMC – Federal Open Market Committee
- FRB – Federal Reserve Bank
- GDP – Gross Domestic Product
- GAO – Government Accountability Office
- GAS – Government Account Series
- GMAC – General Motors Acceptance Corporation

- GOP – Grand Old Party referring to the Republican Party
- GSE – Government-Sponsored Enterprises
- G-S Act – Glass-Steagall Act
- GW – George Walker Bush, 43rd POTUS, also referred to as George W., W., G.W. Bush, Bush Son and Bush Jr.
- HW – George Herbert Walker Bush, 41st POTUS, also referred to as George H.W., George H.W. Bush, H.W., Bush Father and Bush Sr.
- ICE – US Immigration & Customs Enforcement
- IGH – Intra-Governmental Holdings
- IMF – International Monetary Fund
- IRS – Internal Revenue Service
- ISIL – Islamic State of Iraq and the Levant
- ISIS – Islamic State of Iraq and Syria
- LBJ – Lyndon Baines Johnson, 36th POTUS, also referred to as Lyndon B. Johnson and L. Johnson and Johnson.
- MPH – Miles per hour
- MSNBC – Microsoft National Broadcasting Corporation (news outlet which ended its partnership between in 2012 when Comcast bought out Microsoft)
- NASA – National Aeronautics and Space Administration
- NLRA – National Labor Relations Act
- NRA – National Recovery Act
- NYSE – New York Stock Exchange
- NYA – National Youth Administration
- OASI – Old-Age and Survivors Insurance
- OIG – Office of Inspector General
- OK – Okay
- OMB – White House Office of Management and Budget
- POTUS – President of the United States
- PTSD – Post-Traumatic Stress Disorder
- PWA – Public Works Administration
- QE – Quantitative Easing
- S&L – Savings and Loans
- SEC – Securities and Exchange Commission
- SLGS – State and Local Government Series
- SNAP – Supplemental Nutrition Assistance Program
- SOMA – System Open Market Accounts
- SS – Social Security

- SSA – Social Security Act
- SSTF – Social Security Trust Fund
- TIPS – Treasury Inflation-Protected Securities
- TSA – Transportation Security Administration
- UK – United Kingdom
- US – United States of America
- USCG – US Coast Guard
- USCIS – US Citizenship & Immigration Services
- USSS – US Secret Service
- VP – Vice President
- WPA – Works Progress Administration
- WWI – World War I
- WWII – World War II
- Y2K – The year 2000 used in the 1990s to signify the coming turn of the century
- ZIRP – Zero-Interest Rate Policy

List of figures

Preface

We all have that friend. You know the one. The social media savant that posts one hundred and seventeen times a day with political rants that, most of the time, make your skin crawl. You friended them with the best of intentions, you really did. They seemed normal enough at work, perhaps a little quirky but not totally off-the-rails whacked. However, now it is too late. Unsuspectingly, you have friended not one but two of "those friends," and they have become mortal frenemies on your social media continuum: Tanner and Skye. They embody polar opposites on every issue whether socio-economic, political, religious, environmental, or other. Left alone in a sealed room, they would most certainly spontaneously combust in a matter of minutes.

A gun-toting Tea Party ultra-conservative nut, Tanner, borders on the edge of white supremacist racist homophobe. He fills his days and nights listening nonstop to Beck (the radio host not the musician), Limbaugh, and Hannity, then regurgitating the daily dose of right winged rants in an attempt to educate his social media herd on the travesties committed by the Barack Obama administration. He blames the moral decay of America on the elimination of the "under God" clause in the Pledge of Allegiance and lack of prayer in schools. His personal hero and the best President of the United States (POTUS) ever... you guessed it, Ronald Reagan. He recently informed us that we would wrestle away his guns from his cold dead hands while arguing ardently how the AR-15 does not qualify as an automatic assault weapon. His battle cry: "Wake up, America!"

On the other side of the aisle stands Skye – a Pro-Choice, tree-hugging, Bernie-loving, Democratic-Socialist ultra-liberal, or whatever hippies call themselves this week. In her Toms alpargatas, every year she unfailingly dedicates two weeks to voluntourism travel abroad, doing her bit to save the world. She is convinced that Dick Cheney IS the incarnation of the Antichrist and that G.W. had the mental acumen of Forrest Gump (OK, she is probably right about this one). Skye has cried herself to sleep many nights since Jon Stewart retired from The Daily Show. Sure, Trevor Noah seems entertaining enough, but he cannot hold a candle to the pulse his predecessor held on America. A vegan since high school, she took up yoga a few years ago to help her relax. Most recently, her therapist believes that she is suffering from Post-Traumatic Stress Disorder (PTSD) after the 2016 presidential elections.

However, despite Tanner and Skye's shortcomings in regards to open-mindedness, personal hygiene, and shaving habits, they are both uber-informed. Both graduated college and seem very knowledgeable on a broad range of topics. They fill their posts to the brim with facts and figures about their particular cause du jour. Or so we believe, as they relentlessly clog our timeline with memes and headlines replete with data on politics, economics, crime, the environment, ad infinitum. You have seen versions of most of their memes. He will post an unappealing portrait of Barack looking sad and distraught, calling him out on all his supposed fiscal failures. She will counter with a particularly photogenic image of Barack holding hands with Michele, rocking those fabulous guns of hers in an impeccably fitting sleeveless dress, with definitive claims clamoring over his economic successes. They both seem very convincing in their arguments, especially with the high-quality graphics and cool fonts highlighting the key statistical achievements. That is until one stops for a second and questions – where in the heck did they get those facts and, more importantly, how accurate are they?

The Oxford Dictionary defines the words meme and misinformation as:

meme (noun): An image, video, piece of text, or such, sometimes humorous in nature, that is copied and spread rapidly by Internet users, often with slight variations

misinformation (noun): false or inaccurate facts and information, especially that which is deliberately intended to deceive

Buried within the distorted half-truths of his and her memes, both Tanner and Skye present just enough recognizable and accurate claims that make their overall assertions plausible. In a world increasingly filled with "post-truth" politics (Wang, 2016), data and information have taken a back seat to pomp and circumstance. False statistics and fake news spread like wildfire on social media. The prevalent and pervasive practice of jumping to conclusions from supposed self-proclaimed informed consumers, that just glance at a bogus headline without actually reading the article or checking the facts, fuels the misinformation fire like feeding gremlins past midnight. In some cases, by the time the corrected information makes it to the public, no one cares about the truth. Objective facts seem less influential in shaping public opinion than appeals to emotion and personal belief, especially when shared in open social media mass markets.

In this installment of the Misinformation series, we will concentrate on some of the most outrageous socio-economic and politically charged memes posted by Tanner and Skye on the economy of the United States; then we will set the record straight by presenting the data as objectively as possible. We will scatter their meme entries throughout the book, present the real story, then at the end analyze their claims to separate facts from misinformation.

Introduction

"The art of economics consists in looking not merely at the immediate but at the longer effects of any act or policy; it consists in tracing the consequences of that policy not merely for one group but for all groups." (Hazlitt, 1946)

Few things irk engineers and economists more than observing someone draw poor conclusions from perfectly good data. As Mark Twain cleverly stated, "there are lies, damn lies and statistics." Unfortunately, that axiom can ring true when the individual drawing the conclusions manipulates the data or misapplies the statistics. Whether intended deceit from a hidden agenda or technical oversight from lack of understanding the statistical intricacies of a particular analysis, false conclusions can still appear very convincing.

For example, Tanner recently shared a post about a case study of people killed by guns in Australia vs. the US. The author, of this particularly slanted article, claimed that the rate of gun-related deaths Down Under had increased by nearly 25% over a period of four years, from 2011-2014. An avid second amendment supporter, the author made an argument to undermine the success of the Australian gun ban of 1996. What the deceptive or ignorant (or both) author failed to explain was that while the annual number of gun-related deaths had indeed increased from 188 to 230 over a four-year period, the limited portion of data that he had presented did not capture the entire situation. These figures in fact, mathematically accrued to close to 25%, 22.3% to be exact. However, we can file this claim under the category of a grossly misleading statistic.

To prove his point, the biased author cherry-picked the data that supported his hypothesis – a statistical mortal sin. The chart below shows how he purposely selected his mathematically insignificant subset of data to prove his biased viewpoint (the four dark bars on the right of the chart below), and, more importantly, how the full population of data, going back further, supported the complete opposite story. By focusing on a narrow subset of the data then exaggerating by using a percentage (which made the difference look bigger than actual), he pointed out a very impressive, albeit, a very wrong metric – a 25% increase in gun deaths from 2011 to 2014.

Figure 1: Total Gun Deaths in Australia (1980-2014)

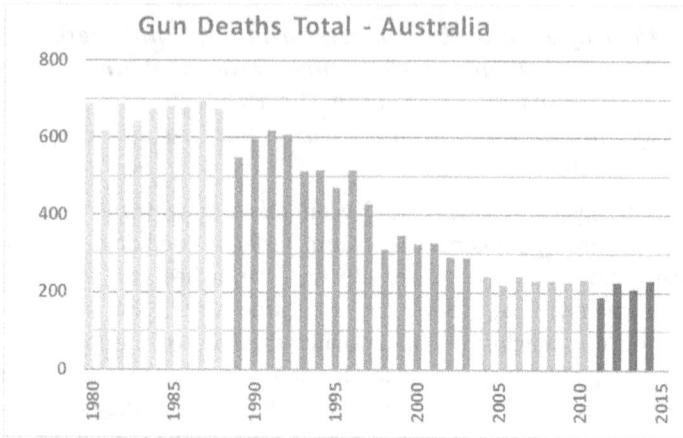

Source: Data from the International Firearm Injury Prevention and Policy

   Looking at the entire progression of the data on the chart, we can draw several mathematically correct conclusions. First, the number of gun-related deaths in Australia has indeed dropped significantly since the ban of 1996. However, the total deaths had already started falling in the late 1980s, pointing to previous events or guns laws that also had a positive effect. Second, the rate had reached a steady state at just over 200 deaths per year over the last decade. Finally, the low point of 188 in 2001 stood as a normal fluctuation of the distribution of the data stream. More specifically, there was no statistical difference in the numbers since 2004. We would expect a slight variation up and down from the mean, and the 188 fell within the "normal" range. Therefore, to claim a rise of 25% since 2011 rated as a "liar liar, pants on fire" on the fib spectrum.

   Taking this example even further, if we analyzed the data for both Australia and the US on a per capita basis going back to 1980 (next chart), we could establish that the Australian levels have dropped by a factor of four since the 1980s. Meanwhile, the US peaked in the early 1990s and then fell steadily to the current value where it has remained flat since 2000, albeit at nearly ten times the Australian rate.

Figure 2: Total Gun Deaths per Capita in Australia and the US (1980-2014)

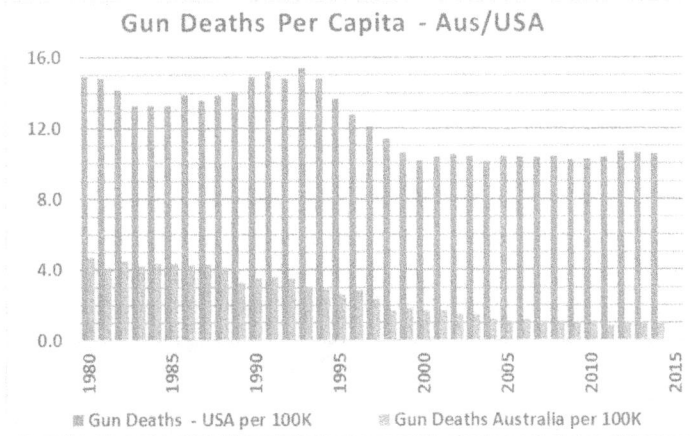

Gun Deaths Per Capita - Aus/USA

Source: Data from the International Firearm Injury Prevention and Policy.

Now, before all the gun-toting second amendment advocates get their panties in a bunch, we show this example to point out how anyone can cherry-pick and manipulate data to prove just about anything. We promise not to take sides in this publication, not even on gun control. At least not until we process the data using robust statistical techniques, such as regression analysis to determine trends and correlations, or Analysis of Variance (ANOVA) to scrutinize and compare different data sets. By relying on raw primary data sources, we will present the impartial facts on some highly volatile subjects so that *we can draw some statistically accurate and unbiased conclusions from the data*. By the way, we will circle back to the gun discussion in a future installment of the "Misinformation" series, which will focus on crime and punishment.

Speaking of neutral vs. prejudiced, with the popularity of social media, just about anyone can offer his or her opinion on any subject seemingly sans consequences. No longer do reporters or newspersons solely report the news. No longer do colleagues and editors of said journalists pour over headlines and articles for accuracy. These days any hack with a blog and a keyboard can spew ignorance, hate, and misconceptions supposedly backed by "data." At last count, Facebook and Twitter had passed the two billion users mark – nearly a third of the world's population. The torrent of ignorant memes and eye-catching headlines, from fake news sites and bloggers with an ax to grind, stream endlessly on social network timelines. Case in point, a recent popular meme on social media, posted by Skye of course, clamored on the economic success of the sitting president in comparison to the failures of his predecessor. In reality, once we analyzed the raw data, both Commanders in Chief had little influence on most of the financial claims from the meme.

The assertions made in this post from Skye focused the rise of the stock market, the increase in the Gross Domestic Product (GDP), the reduction in the unemployment rate, and other such statistics. Unfortunately, outside factors can dominate economic indicators in ways that far exceed the influence exerted by a particular presidency. Moreover, while some decisions made in the White House can affect the economy in a profound way, typically, the changes rarely manifest themselves during the same term(s) of a president.

Case in point, the steady deregulation of the Savings & Loans (S&L) banking industry in the 1980s and 1990s, eventually led to the repeal of the Glass–Steagall Act in 1999, during the Bill Clinton administration. This repeal would set off a domino effect that would implode a decade later in the housing and lending crash of 2008. G.W. Bush inherited the blame in the last year of his second term and B. Obama the brunt of its consequence, i.e., the Wall Street bailout, in his first day in office. "Welcome to the White House, Mr. President, have a nice day."

A booby trap set ten years prior dominated the economic landscape, scurrying party line Democrats to blame George W. immediately, when in fact, he had nothing to do with the chain of events that brought on the housing crash. Now, let's not pull a Pontius Pilate on G.W. Bush and cleanse his hands of all blame. From an economic point of view, Jr. buried the country in record debt from what started as a justified War on Terror in Afghanistan, then extended it with a fabricated reason for going to war against Iraq, a country that had nothing to do with the initial terrorist attack. The after effects of two unrelated events, S&L deregulation and then the attacks of September 11, combined almost a decade later into a perfect economic storm dubbed The Great Recession.

In this book, as we delve into key economic and financial topics, we will shed light on the fiscal assertions of some of the most egregious meme allegations from Tanner and Skye. We will reconstruct some of the more critical economic indexes into their fundamental components and then analyze the data by political party, by president, and by other significant causes. We will find out if, in fact, there is any link to the Democrat vs. Republican claims that their party holds the key to economic and monetary progress.

We will also tackle a host of other socio-economic and politically charged issues. For example, did the New Deal incentivize the country out of The Great Depression or did the beginning of welfare entitlement prolong the economic downturn of The Great Depression? Did Voodoo Economics, a term attributed to George H.W. Bush when he was running against Ronald Reagan for the 1980 Republican nomination, start the clock on what has become the pink elephant in the room – a national debt of nearly 20 trillion dollars? Is Obamacare to blame for the doubling of the debt over the last few years? How much have we spent on Health Care and are we actually helping those previously uninsured? Or, are we instead drowning in military debt facilitated courtesy of Bush Father & Son? And speaking of the debt, to whom do we owe it? Whose rich uncle has been enabling our insatiable thirst to spend more than we earn? Alternatively, with what seems to be the pervasive attitude in DC, does the debt even matter? No one seems to understand fully this debt and deficit stuff anyways. One day, will we just pretend the debt never existed? Or perhaps, we could just print more money and wipe it away, starting over with a clean slate. If only.

Now, before we get started, let's discuss a couple of key items that affect any discussion on these types of highly volatile topics – sources of data and personal affiliations. The data mined for this book comes strictly from primary sources that publish raw data to keep from falling into a fact checking Catch-22. For example, the latest craze in the supposed pursuit of truth comes in the form of political fact checking. Many "fair and balanced" outlets research candidate claims then rate them from "Gandhi" truthful to "Joe Isuzu" falsehood. Which sounds great in theory, until a check on the checkers exposed that some of the supposed fair and impartial assessments were perhaps not as neutral as advertised (Roff, 2013). To avoid this trap, for our analysis, we will strictly draw raw data from reputable primary sources, which we have in abundance because we live in a free country, and because of unrelenting pioneer activists such as Ralph Nader, who have continually pushed our government for more transparency.

Our federal government releases endless reams of information and documents, making it readily available to uber-geeks (like me) that are willing to dig through bottomless pits of published data, charts, and graphs. Much to the chagrin of J. Edgar Hoover, the first Freedom of Information Act of 1966 along with multiple amendments and additional measures such as the Electronic Freedom of Information Act Amendments of 1996, assure that we have access to government data, particularly as it relates to finances. Most of the sources for information used for this book include official documents published online by the Congressional Budget Office (CBO), the White House Office of Management and Budget (OMB), the Bureau of Labor Statistics (BLS), The US Department of the Treasury, and other similar outlets. If we reference data from another source, we will check it for accuracy as best we can and then label it as such.

As far as personal affiliations, the fiscally conservative yet socially tolerant author has plenty of strong opinions on the issues and the candidates he supports; just ask his social media network of friends. However, for this book, he has set those aside and focused solely on the data. As you read along you will notice shots fired on both sides of the aisle and even an occasional quip about third party candidates – such as the size of Ross Perot's ears, Ralph Nader's insatiable thirst to save the world or the rumor that Gary Johnson climbed Mr. Everest with a hookah in his backpack. There exists too much material, chicanery, and nonsense from all sides to pass up a laugh or two at the expense of any politician, regardless of party membership.

Finally, for 99-percentile commoners like us, it is hard to wrap our heads around the gargantuan size of the federal budget. Unless you hang with Warren Buffet, Bill Gates or Mark Zuckerberg on a regular basis, who the heck has a feel for spending in the millions, billions or especially trillions of dollars. To gain insight on the size and breadth of the federal budget, we will occasionally reference the government's revenue and spending relative to that of a typical American household. Our representative family, Jonathan and Maria Barleycorn, joined in marriage nearly 20 years ago, and live in Middletown America with two kids, Frank, a sophomore in college, and Roxy, a junior in high school. Jonathan works as a shift supervisor at the local food processing plant while Maria recently received a promotion from receptionist to office manager at a large insurance office. Combined they make $56k per year. After saving for a few years, they recently bought the house of their dreams, a $170k single-family home. Jonathan has stashed some money away for retirement through the 401k account offered by his company. However, a few years ago, he suffered through a corporate downsizing and remained jobless for nine months. This set the Barleycorns way back on their credit cards balances, and they still owe several creditors a total of nearly $20k. During the worst of the unemployment stretch, they even had to borrow from his retirement account to pay for their monthly obligations – the mortgage, two car payments, Frank's college tuition, and Roxy's music lessons. Throughout the book, we will discover plenty of similarities between our struggling family, the Barleycorns, and the financial state of the federal government.

So, enough with the intro, let's get started.

Chapter 1

National Debt

TANNER VS. SKYE: We have had a flurry of social media activity since last night. It started innocently enough with an unsuspecting third party facetiously mentioning Obamacare in a post about the high cost of insurance. Tanner quickly chimed in with his usual 6-paragraph bully dissertation on B. Obama's economic shortcomings, crushing the thread. Or so he thought. Not to be outdone, Skye countered quickly with several short responses attacking most of his claims then outflanking him by presenting various pro-Obama factoids of her own. By the second hour, the tone of the postings had escalated into an angry discourse between seasoned gladiators. Neither would give an inch – not tonight.

The battle between Tanner and Skye spilled over into several other posts that extended into the morning. Each picked up right where he or she left off, which eventually led to the following meme postings from our protagonists. Tanner attacked B. Obama's national debt record, calling the president out on his favorite litany of wrongdoings: doubling the debt, bankrupting the Social Security fund, overspending on standard liberal welfare policy and mortgaging the future of our country. Skye focused like a laser on B. Obama's record on improved economic indexes – the doubling of the Dow Jones Industrial Average (DJIA), the growth of the GDP, the lowering of the deficit and the decrease in the unemployment rate. Both sounded very convincing, but how do we know who's right and who's wrong?

Figure 3: Meme entries from Tanner and Skye on the performance of B. Obama

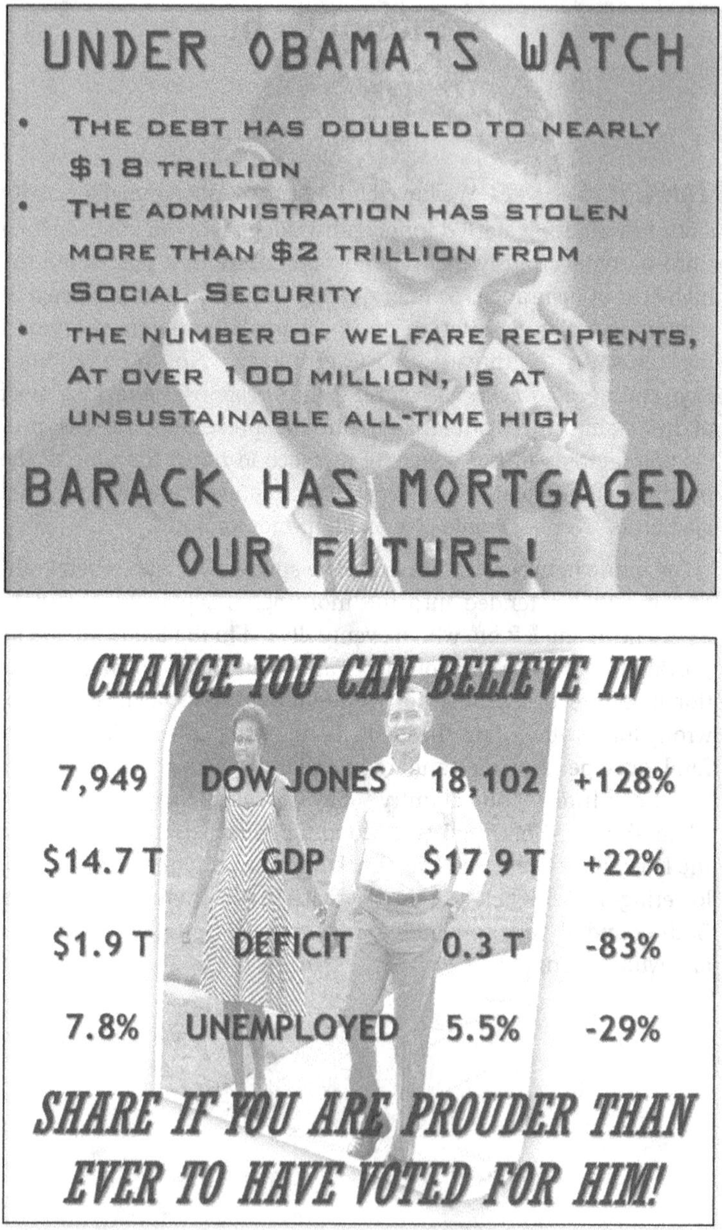

UNDER OBAMA'S WATCH

- THE DEBT HAS DOUBLED TO NEARLY $18 TRILLION
- THE ADMINISTRATION HAS STOLEN MORE THAN $2 TRILLION FROM SOCIAL SECURITY
- THE NUMBER OF WELFARE RECIPIENTS, AT OVER 100 MILLION, IS AT UNSUSTAINABLE ALL-TIME HIGH

BARACK HAS MORTGAGED OUR FUTURE!

CHANGE YOU CAN BELIEVE IN

7,949	DOW JONES	18,102	+128%
$14.7 T	GDP	$17.9 T	+22%
$1.9 T	DEFICIT	0.3 T	-83%
7.8%	UNEMPLOYED	5.5%	-29%

SHARE IF YOU ARE PROUDER THAN EVER TO HAVE VOTED FOR HIM!

Source: Adapted from popular social media memes

THE REAL STORY: Few subjects receive more confusing coverage in the media and press than the national debt, often mixed up with the annual budget deficit. Both political parties report convenient subsets of fiscal debt and deficit data to support their agenda and candidates – that we expect. However, even reputable news outlets routinely publish articles on the national debt that leave us perplexed, scratching our heads.

One of the more recent egregious cases of overt muddying came from a reputable cable news outlet headline that read: "Deficit shrinks by $1 trillion in B. Obama era" (Benen, 2015). That statement, on its own, stands as factually correct. However, what is unclear and confusing to the common public from the headline of the article is that the $1 trillion dollars are actually a cumulative reduction in *deficit overspending* of the annual federal budget and not the national debt. It would be akin to claiming that, even though the Barleycorns owe Visa and their other credit cards a principal balance of $20,000, this month they only added $1,000 to the overall balance instead of $2,000 like last month. In both cases, the credit card balances continued to grow, but they did, in fact, reduce the overspending this month by $1,000. Yeah, team!

As anyone who has ever carried a large credit card balance can attest, this is a losing proposition for Jonathan and Maria, as the interest will eat them up alive. This credit card spending game becomes a vicious cycle for them as their monthly budget barely covers the interest charges, which prevents them from lower the principal balances. The principal amount continues to rise, forcing the cardholders to request higher and higher spending limits and to apply for more credit cards. The creditors, in turn, continue to increase the credit limits and grant them more cards, as they know that they have their claws grasped firmly on their prey. Accordingly, as the principal balances on multiple credit cards increase, the monthly interest payments continue to climb as the total debt grows, further limiting the ability to pay down the principal balances. Their creditors got 'em, and the cycle keeps repeating itself.

Does this scenario sound familiar? Well, that analogy is not drastically different from what has transpired with the US national debt, ballooning to nearly $20 trillion over the last four decades. In 2015, the government paid $223 billion in debt interest payments alone. For those scoring at home, that represents more money than we spent on Education, Environment, Space & Technology, Agriculture and Energy _combined_ in the 2015 fiscal year. Let that insanity sink in for a minute. Common sense would dictate that this house of cards will come crashing down at some point, right? However, before we draw any conclusions, let's first analyze the impact of the chronic overspending in Washington. Then we can discuss the merits of the oft-mentioned solution of a balanced budget amendment and how to pay down the national debt.

In the credit card analogy of the Barleycorns, the owner of the debt often ends up declaring bankruptcy, also known as defaulting on their loans. Alternatively, they may clean up their act by consolidating debt, getting the overspending reasonably under control and then paying it off little by little. The cases of Greece in the last decade and Mexico in the 1980s and 1990s ring familiar for both of these scenarios, respectively. We will break down in detail where the US stands in this ugly situation but first, let's start with some financial basics and a brief historical summary of the debt.

Debt vs. deficit

Let's begin by defining two terms routinely mixed up and misused – deficit and debt. A budget deficit arises when the federal government spends more than it earns in revenue in a given year. We call the opposite of a budget deficit a surplus. The accrual of annual surpluses and deficits going back to the Revolutionary War constitutes the national debt. Therefore, when we mention a deficit (or a surplus), we denote an annual occurrence. When we allude to the debt, we mean the aggregate sum of all the surpluses and deficits.

Next, the national debt consists of two primary buckets: Public Debt and Intra-Governmental Holdings (IGH). The public portion includes debt held by the US public (individuals, banks, mutual funds, and such) and outside entities (other countries and foreign investors), in Treasury bills, notes, savings bonds and such. The IGH debt comes from money borrowed from other government entities, 58.1% of which originates from that seemingly endless cash cow known as the Social Security trust fund. The list below shows how six funds hold over 90% of the total owed to the 131 total funds that make up the IGH. Social Security consists of two funds – the Federal Old-Age and Survivors Insurance (OASI) and the Federal Disability Insurance Trust Funds (*in italics in the list*).

Figure 4: List of Intra-Governmental Holdings Trust Funds

No	Name	Percent
1	*Federal Old-Age and Survivors Insurance Trust Fund*	56.0%
2	Civil Service Retirement and Disability Fund, Office of Personnel Mgt	15.0%
3	Department of Defense, Military Retirement Fund	8.9%
4	Federal Hospital Insurance Trust Fund	4.3%
5	Department of Defense, Medicare Eligible Retiree Fund	4.0%
6	*Federal Disability Insurance Trust Fund*	2.1%
11	Other 125 Funds Combined	9.6%

Source: Data from the Department of the Treasury, Federal Reserve Board

The next couple of charts shows the US national debt and the annual Surplus or Deficit since 1970. We chose 1970 to simplify the scale of this graph. Barring three small blips of around $60 billion during WWII (1943-45), the deficit numbers since 1970, in the hundreds of billions and trillions of dollars, dwarf the collective spending of the previous 200 years. Something else happened in 1971 that also directly affected the growth of the debt since then, and we will cover that at length in another section.

In the following chart, we can identify how the national debt, and especially borrowing from IGH, began in earnest in the 1980s. The amount and percent of the IGH portion grew steadily and had accounted for about 30% of the overall debt over the last decade.

Figure 5: US National Debt – Public vs. IGH (1970-2015)

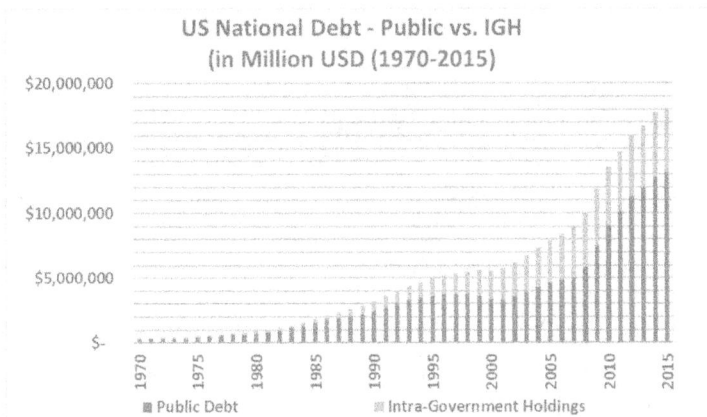

Source: Data from the White House Office of Management and Budget, Table 7.1 - Federal Debt at the End of the Year 1940-2021

In the Surplus/Deficit chart below, when we break down the contribution by the presidents since 1970, B. Obama owns the six highest deficits ever on record by a long shot. However, as we pointed out earlier, let's not ignore that he inherited the housing mess left behind by B. Clinton. For the first three years in office, through no fault of his own, Barack's budget included the massive Wall Street bailout, peaking in 2009 with a record $1.9 trillion deficit. However, don't get too excited if you are a card-carrying member of the GOP siding with Tanner on his anti "libtard" rants (he claims he invented the derogatory term for mentally deficient liberals). B. Obama's predecessor, George W., owned the five previous highest annual deficits. And, by the way, technically W. owns the gargantuan 2009 deficit, even though it falls under B. Obama's watch since the annual budget receives approval from Congress the previous year.

Figure 6: US Surplus/Deficits – Public vs. IGH (1970-2015)

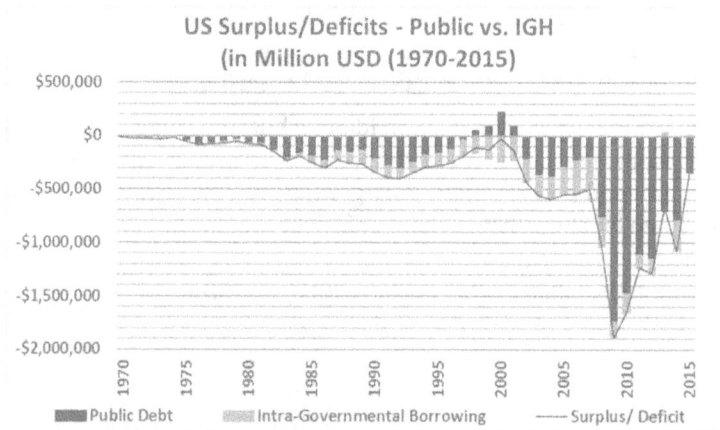

Source: Data from the White House Office of Management and Budget, Table 7.1 - Federal Debt at the End of the Year 1940-2021

Looking only at the Surplus/Deficit chart, it would make sense to infer that after modest deficits by J. Carter in the second half of the 1970s, that R. Reagan and G.W.H. Bush drove annual deficits into the 1990s; then B. Clinton pushed it down to an almost balanced budget by 2000. Yeah, Bill!

However, what we cannot appreciate from only looking at the previous debt and deficit charts is that Bill presided over the last relatively peaceful stretch in US history, bookended by the First Iraq War under Bush Sr. and the War on Terror by Bush Jr.

After a quick and decisive win over Saddam Hussein and his vaunted Iraqi Republican Guard, General Colin Powell encouraged G.W.H. Bush to ratchet down the military spend in his last two years in office, much to the chagrin of then Secretary of Defense Dick Cheney. B. Clinton built on this "peace dividend" momentum to maintain the lowest military budget of any administration since WWII. More importantly, Bush Sr. committed political suicide by backing down from his famous "read my lips" campaign promise and raised taxes, which paved the way for what happened next – the stock market exploded in the late 1990s with the rise of tech companies and the dot-com bubble.

The tech boom brought in hundreds of millions of dollars of unanticipated tax revenue on capital gains and an increased job market with higher wages from tech jobs. Neither a Pee Wee Herman White House administration nor a Bernie Sander's Democratic-Socialist agenda of "free stuff for everyone" could have derailed the unprecedented growth of the DJIA or the GDP runaway freight trains of the 1990s.

Figure 7: Dow Jones Industrial Average, 1970 to Present

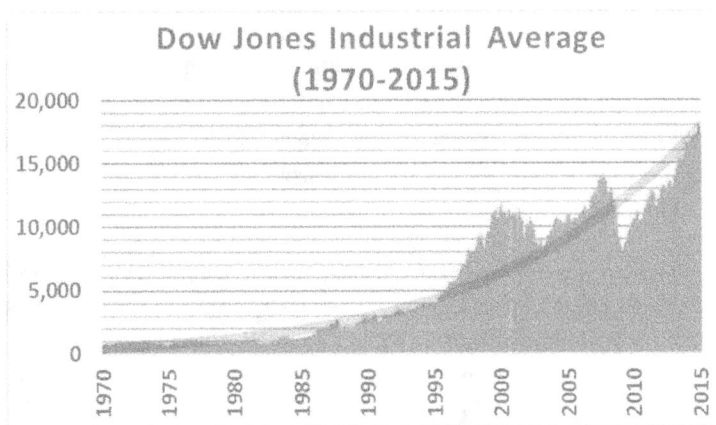

Source: Data from Williamson (2016), Measuring Worth, Daily Closing Values of the DJA in the United States, 1885 to Present

Figure 8: US Gross Domestic Product (1970-2015)

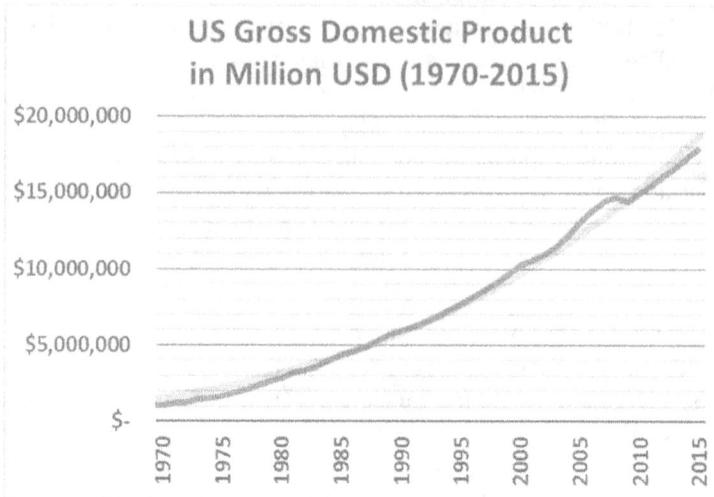

US Gross Domestic Product in Million USD (1970-2015)

Source: Data from the Congressional Budget Office, Potential GDP 1949-2026

The previous charts show the DJIA and GDP since 1970 with trend lines. The huge mound in the volatile DJIA, from 1995-2003 and above the trend line, shows the rise then fall of tech. A few years later, 2008, the market fell off a precipice then fought its way back to get on track by 2014.

While on the subject of Bill Clinton, let's set the record straight on his supposed balanced budgets and surpluses – one of Skye's favorite talking points when paying homage to Bill. _B. Clinton never actually balanced the budget nor did he incur a surplus during any of the fiscal years of his tenure_ (Steiner, 2011). In typical Washington double-speak, the White House residents, pounding their chests with pride while taking credit for balancing the budget, conveniently excluded the intra-governmental holdings in their deficit calculation. In one of Washington's dirty little secrets, the OMB only reports the public debt in the annual budget tables, while conveniently disclosing the total debt, inclusive of the intra-governmental holdings, in another report. Using that type of misleading accounting, anyone can claim a surplus if he or she leaves out a portion of what he or she owes. It would be similar to the Barleycorn family analogy if they did not include the money they had borrowed from their 401k in their household balance sheet. In B. Clinton's case, the Surplus/Deficit chart shows the public debt climbing past the Mendoza line into positive territory (four bars from 1998-2001) while the IGH drags it back down to the real negative deficit.

Slick Willie paid down the public debt by borrowing from Social Security and other Trust Funds to make his numbers look good. In 2000, for example, Social Security accounted for $150.2 of the $248.7 billion borrowed from intra-governmental holdings. Therefore, while the White House claimed surpluses of $51.2, $88.7, $222.6, and $90.2 billion from 1998 to 2001, actually we incurred deficits of $109.0, $127.3, $23.2, and $141.2 billion, respectively. Now you know.

(ASIDE: Giving credit to Bill Clinton for "fixing" the economy in the 1990s is akin to crediting Ronald Reagan for "taking down" the Berlin Wall. Both just happened to preside at the specific moment of historical events. Seventy years of a failed, and abusive communist experiment collapsed the United Soviet Socialist Republic. However, ask Tanner and any of his card-carrying Republican friends and they will swear that R. Reagan single-handedly collapsed the Soviet Union with his strong military policy and anti-communist rhetoric. His "Mr. Gorbachev, tear down this wall" speech made for great press, sound bites, and future memes, but that is about it. But enough ranting, let's get back to the thread.)

The G.W. administration kicked-off with a carryover of the late 1990s exuberance; then everything went south quickly as the dot-com bubble burst and terrorists flew planes into the World Trade Center twin towers, the Pentagon, and a field in Pennsylvania. Military spending on two wars, in Afghanistan then Iraq, and the foundation of the Department of Homeland Security overextended the budget, and for most of the balance of his terms, G.W. Bush ran more than a half trillion dollar annual deficit. The deficit ballooned in his last year in office, signaling the beginning of the market crash bailout.

B. Obama, as we mentioned before, inherited a nightmare scenario – two wars, The Great Recession, and the Wall Street Bailout, all of which wreaked havoc with his budgets in his first term in office and led to five consecutive years of deficits of more than a trillion dollars. While he ended the wars in Iraq and Afghanistan, the military expenditure was not reduced drastically due to the continuing unrest in the Middle East and the rise of ISIS (Islamic State of Iraq and Syria), or ISIL (Islamic State of Iraq and the Levant), as he refers to them. Also, his crowning achievement, the Affordable Care Act, i.e., Obamacare, kicked into gear in 2011. By the start of his second term, he had managed to slow down the bleeding (overspending deficit), but not quite to the level of Bush Jr. By 2015, a continuing recipe of more revenue from increased taxes, a zero-interest rate policy (ZIRP) by Fed and an increase in consumption lowered the deficit to $326 billion, but it quickly climbed back to an expected ~$600 billion deficit in 2016.

While easy to assign blame to several presidents based on the massive overspending since the 1970s, we need to temper the haste with which we accuse them. Any discussion on the debt and deficit needs to be framed by the GDP. As we pointed out on the charts earlier, the massive growth of the DJIA and GDP over time makes presidential comparisons highly unfair. Just about every president will spend more than his predecessor due to the exponential growth of the economy. So instead, we need to focus on the percentage of the debt/deficits relative to the GDP. This presents a more balanced view of how administrations focused their spending. We will come back to this subject later, in the chapter on comparisons by party and president. But first, let's take a quick stroll through time and double click on the history of the debt.

Chapter 2

Progression of the debt

We can trace the national debt back to the Revolutionary War. By 1790, the earliest available records from the Congressional Budget Office, the fight for independence had set the newly formed country of the United States of America back $71 million. Think of it as the price of admission into a fancy Country Club (pun intended). Plotting the aggregate debt on a log scale chart, we can identify some key milestones in the ever-growing national debt.

Figure 9: US National Debt (1790-2015)

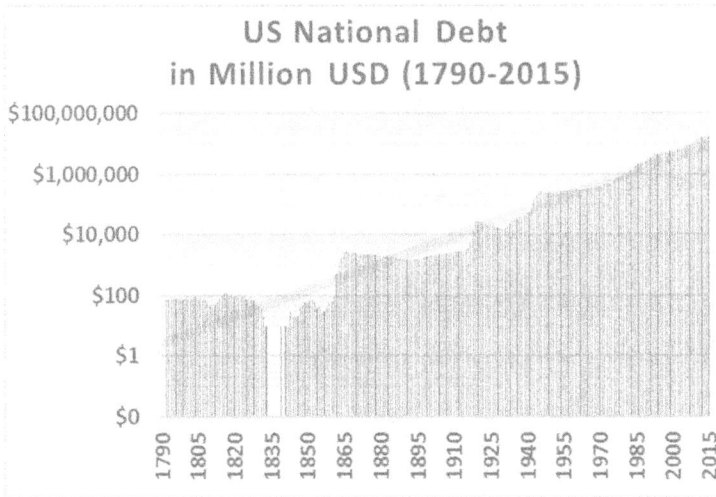

Source: Data from the White House Office of Management and Budget, Table 1.1 - Summary of Receipts, Outlays, Surpluses, and Deficits 1789-2021

Starting at $71 million in 1790, the debt stayed relatively flat for two decades, until the War of 1812 pushed it past $100 million. By 1835, we had just about paid off the debt, down to a measly $33K, under the leadership (closer to obsession) of Andrew Jackson (Smith, 2011). However, that lasted about 30 milliseconds. A depression period ensued, which some blamed on Jackson's frugal ways, even refusing to invest in new highways for a quickly expanding nation. Slowly, the government undid most of Jackson's hard work over the next 25 years, setting the debt back to $64 million by 1860.

The outbreak of the Civil War set new heights for the debt, driving it well over the $1 billion threshold. We kept the debt in check for the next five decades and then The First World War came along, raising the bar over $10 billion. Twenty years passed and, after a decade of mounting debt from The Great Depression, World War II pushed it over $100 billion. After a few years of nearly balanced budgets in the post-war glee and prosperity, the debt began to rise slowly again, first during the Korean War in the 1950s, then the Cold War and the Vietnam War into the 1960s and 1970s. By 1980s, amid a recession period after an oil crunch and The Great Inflation, R. Reagan crossed over the $1 trillion marker with his philosophy of a strong military, fueled by his Star Wars initiative. Bush Sr. then extended the streak with the first Iraq War. After an overspending slowdown in the second half of the 1990s, the aggregate debt continued to rise exponentially after the attack on September 11, 2001, and the ensuing War on Terror. Finally, with the housing crash of 2008, the subsequent recession and Obamacare, we accelerated past the $10 trillion mark. On its current course, the national debt will scream past the $20 trillion mark in the fiscal year 2017.

Surpluses & deficits

Looking at the debt from an annual budgetary angle, after the initial expenditure for independence, our founding fathers, followed by seven decades of presidents, adhered mostly to an overall balanced budget. The debt started at $71 million, peaked at $127 million during the War of 1812, bottomed out at $33K in 1835, and then by 1860 had grown back to $64 million.

Figure 10: US Debt – Annual Balance (1790-1860)

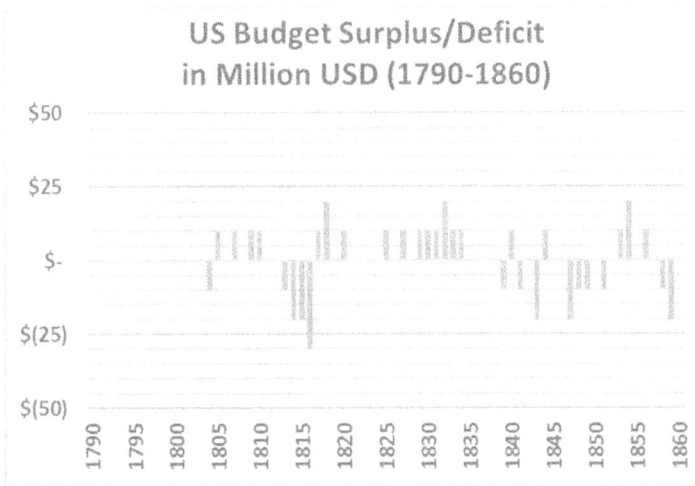

US Budget Surplus/Deficit in Million USD (1790-1860)

Source: Data from the White House Office of Management and Budget, Table 1.1 - Summary of Receipts, Outlays, Surpluses, and Deficits 1789-2021

The annual budget stood on the surplus side in 41 of those 70 years, virtually even-steven up to that point. Which in retrospect, looms as a considerable achievement bearing in mind that the number of states in the Union had more than doubled, from 13 to 33, and that the population had increased tenfold, from 3 to 30 million, since the Declaration of Independence in 1776.

After the Civil War had pushed the debt to $2.7 billion, the next 40 years brought prosperity, surpluses, and only 11 annual deficits, leading to the Spanish-American War in 1898. From then until 1910, just before the First World War, only two years enjoyed a surplus. By then, the US had grown to 46 states with a census nearing 100 million.

Figure 11: US Debt – Annual Balance (1860-1910)

Source: Data from the White House Office of Management and Budget,
Table 1.1 - Summary of Receipts, Outlays, Surpluses, and Deficits 1789-2021

World War I forced three years of deficits, then the Roaring 1920s
generated an entire decade of federal surpluses and joyful Charles-
ton-dancing fools. However, the hammer fell in 1929 on Black
Thursday, kicking off the start of The Great Depression. From 1931 to
the end of the Second World War in 1945, the US drowned in annual
deficits from New Deal social programs and military spending.

Figure 12: US Debt – Annual Balance (1910-1970)

Source: Data from the White House Office of Management and Budget,
Table 1.1 - Summary of Receipts, Outlays, Surpluses, and Deficits 1789-2021

The period from post-WWII until the end of the 1960s produced only six years of plus-side budgets, and Richard Nixon's first year in office, 1969, stands as the last time we sniffed an annual surplus.

Since 1970, the closest the US has come to a balanced budget was in 2000, after the prosperity of the dot-com bubble of the 1990s. We only had a $17.9 billion deficit that year, which seems like a lot, but in the current currency of deficits in the trillions of dollars, that appears like a bargain now. Note that we had to plot the surpluses/deficits in four different charts because the scale of the budget has grown so much and the first three charts, in the millions and billions of dollars, would disappear in the noise of the last graph, in the trillions of dollars.

Figure 13: US Debt – Annual Balance (1970-2015)

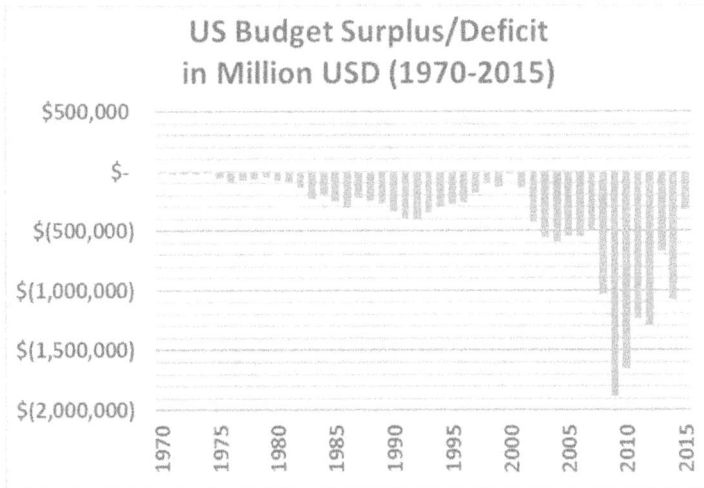

Source: Data from the White House Office of Management and Budget, Table 1.1 - Summary of Receipts, Outlays, Surpluses, and Deficits 1789-2021.

OK, it does not take a genius to figure out that wars, especially big wars, have an enormous impact on the national debt and the annual budget surpluses and deficits. Wars, so far, have raised the ceiling on the debt in a consistent step-function pattern that has yet to retreat. Other large-scale economic events have also moved the needle on the debt both in positive and negative directions. Postwar prosperity triggered economic upticks after the Civil War, WWI, and WWII that held back the growth of the debt and even reduced it, albeit for brief periods. The tech boom of the 1990s also moved the needle, bringing the deficit back to an almost balanced state.

On the other side of the coin, The Great Depression, the 1970s Oil Crunch, The Great Inflation, and the Housing Crash of 2008 caused temporary distortions in the debt continuum that quickly corrected back to the trend of exponential growth. We have increasingly gone from budgets in the millions to the billions and now in the trillions. Where is all this money coming from and how do we pay for these increasingly alarming expenditures?

Chapter 3

Sources of revenue

So how does the federal government make money? Well, good question. They tax us and place tariffs on goods imported from other nations. Our taxation history goes back to the colonial days. We did not take kindly to taxation without representation, so much so, that we went to war against the British Empire to gain our independence. Well, that and for the right to buy a decent cup of tea at a fair price in Boston.

After the Revolutionary War, to run the newly established government, our founding fathers relied on taxing mostly goods – alcohol, sugar, tobacco, property, and even slaves. To fund the War of 1812, the government resorted to taxing additional goods such as precious metals and implementing tariffs on imported goods. Four scores later, the Civil War raised the bar on government expenses, forcing the Union to pass additional measures and the first temporary income tax laws went into effect. They even appointed a Commissioner of Internal Revenue to enforce the tax laws by seizing property and prosecuting violators. While famously credited for abolishing slavery, in 1862, Lincoln founded what became the precursor to an infamous American establishment that will last for as long we have a need for governmental oversight – the Bureau of Internal Revenue, later renamed the Internal Revenue Service (IRS) in the 1950s.

After the Civil War, in 1872, the income tax gave way to increased taxes on existing goods. In an attempt by the government to resurrect the income tax in the 1890s, in order to raise more dollars to keep up with the quickly growing nation, the Supreme Court found income tax unconstitutional due to lack of disparate apportionment among states. So how do you circumvent an unconstitutional tax? You write it into the US Constitution, duh! In 1913, and just in time for World War I, the 16th Amendment passed into law. The first Form 1040 went into effect, making income taxes for individuals and corporations a permanent thorn in our collective sides.

(_ASIDE_: Besides the 16th Amendment, another important event occurred in 1913 – the formation of the Federal Reserve System, i.e., the Central Bank of the United States. The combination of these two historical events gave access to unprecedented funds to both the executive and legislative branches of the government and a piggy bank with which to play. We will circle back to this thread a little later when we discuss the events that facilitated our runaway ~$20 trillion national debt.)

Three decades later, amid World War II, the withholding tax law went into effect, successfully increasing the number of taxpayers and revenue to new heights by passing on the reporting of all wage earners to businesses. No longer could potential taxpayers disregard filing their taxes nor companies pay them under the table without the risk of incurring the wrath of the IRS. Al Capone learned this lesson the hard way. Since the 1980s and in the name of fiscal restructuring, every president has gotten into the act, implementing various tax reforms, reconciliation, and relief laws, which Congress passed into the books.

Figure 14: Sources of Federal Revenue – 2015

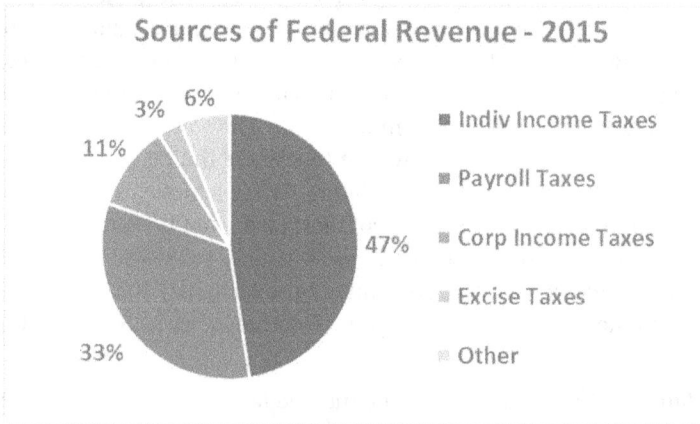

Sources of Federal Revenue - 2015

- Indiv Income Taxes — 47%
- Payroll Taxes — 33%
- Corp Income Taxes — 11%
- Excise Taxes — 3%
- Other — 6%

Source: Data from the White House Office of Management and Budget, Table 2.1 – Receipts by Source

In 2015, about half (47%) of the revenue collected by the feds came from individual income taxes. The second highest source, 33%, arose in the form of payroll taxes – those irritating deductions that show up in our payroll stubs labeled Social Security, Medicare, and unemployment. Corporate taxes only constituted 11%, while the excise bucket generated 3% of the revenue from commodities such as tobacco, alcohol, and gas. Excise is a fancy word for anything that the government wants to profit from or discourage consumption. The "Other" pile includes estate taxes, gift taxes, profits from federal assets, regulatory fees, and accounted for the last 6% of the federal income.

Effective tax rates

The US implements a progressive tax system which means that we pay more as we earn more. The hypothetical chart below shows the difference in total income taxes paid between a progressive and a proportional tax system.

Figure 15: Progressive vs. Proportional Tax System

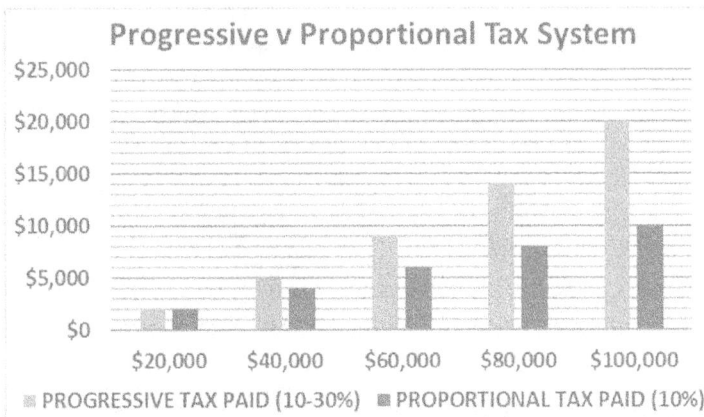

Source: Hypothetical example

In this fictitious example, five persons earn $20k to $100k in $20k increments. The government taxes first $20k at 10%. Each additional $20k in income after that earned gets taxed at an additional 5% tax rate so that the top bracket, in the case, pays 30%. When compared to a proportional 10% tax system, the top earners pay twice as much tax in the progressive system.

This overly simplified explanation is not drastically different from our current system, even though, the tax brackets and tax rates have changed numerous times over the years (Tax Foundation, 2013). In 2015, the lowest bracket paid 10% and the highest 39.6%.

Something caught our attention in that last section on sources of revenue – why did corporations only pay 11% of the total tax revenue but individuals paid 47%? Is corporate America not carrying their fair share of income taxes? Skye has been harping for years on the unfair tax breaks for one-percenters and huge corporations.

She recently hammered Donald Trump mercilessly for boasting in a presidential debate about how "he is smart" for not paying income taxes. She then went after Apple for avoiding taxes by playing the offshore shelter game. By the way, how "The Donald" ended up in a debate as one of two presidential finalists, then wound up winning the election in an unpredictable and unprecedented upset, is a topic for a whole series of books… really thick books.

First, let's not confuse the percentage of revenues collected to applicable tax brackets for individuals and corporations. Per the IRS, they received 148.8 million individual tax returns in 2015. Currently, the lowest tax rate starts at 10% for a single taxpayer with income below $9.3k and the highest tops out at 39.6% for income above $415k. Married couples filing jointly pay similar rates – 10% below $18.6k and 39.6% above $467k. Conversely, corporations filed 10.8 million returns. The federal tax rate for corporations starts at 15% below $50k in revenue and quickly grows to 34% above $100k, maxing out at 35% above $18.3 million. However, *neither individuals nor corporations pay anywhere near those rates due to tax breaks, deductions, credits, etc.*

The IRS publishes detailed income tax return data for individuals and corporations going back to 1996 so we can reverse engineer the actual tax rates by brackets. Since the corporate tax returns lag the individual returns by a year, we based the following analysis on taxes filed from 1996-2013 and 1996-2014, respectively, the last year with complete data for both. We would have preferred for the bracketed data to go back further, say 1930, to see how the contributions from the brackets have changed over time. However, even though the data only goes back 20 years, we can still observe significant changes in tax rates and bracket contributions.

In 2013, the effective tax rates for individuals grew progressively larger as the brackets increased per the previous chart. Surprisingly, that was not the case 20 years ago, when the bottom three brackets, grossing $20k and less, paid more than the fourth bracket. The poorest folks, $5k and below, spent an insane 17% of their earnings in taxes – talk about adding insult to injury. By 2004, George W. had corrected that situation and the bottom six brackets all paid less than 10% tax. On the other end of the scale, the top bracket, defined as $1 million or more, paid less than 30% from 2002-2012, but B. Obama fixed that, and now their effective rate is at 32%, back to the pre-2002 level.

Figure 16: Individual Effective Tax Rates (1996-2014)

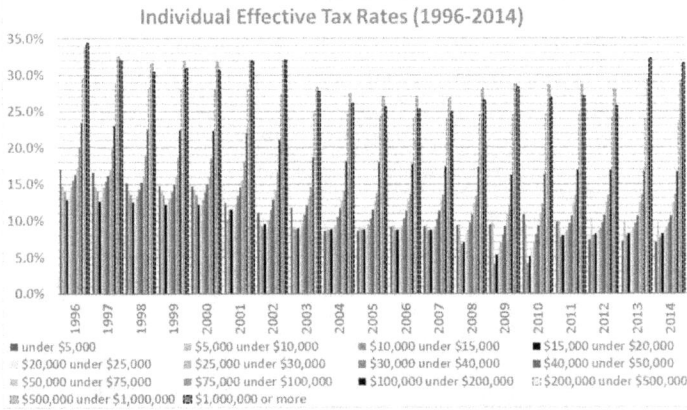

Source: Data from the IRS, Table 1.2 All Returns: Adjusted Gross Income, Exemptions, Deductions, and Tax Items 1996-2013, Individual Income Tax Return

Figure 17: Individual Income Tax Percent Contribution (1996-2014)

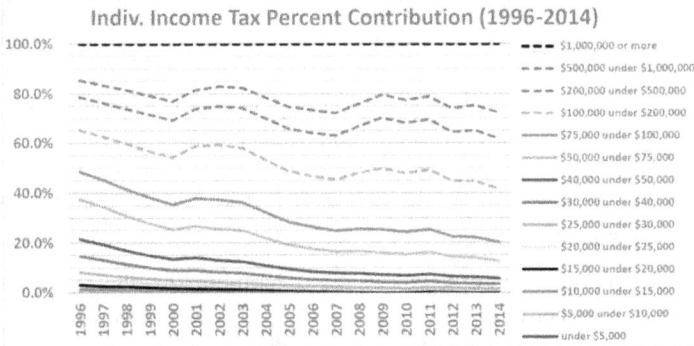

Source: Data from the IRS, Table 1.2 All Returns: Adjusted Gross Income, Exemptions, Deductions, and Tax Items 1996-2013, Individual Income Tax Return

Figure 18: Individual Income Tax Paid in Million USD (1996-2014)

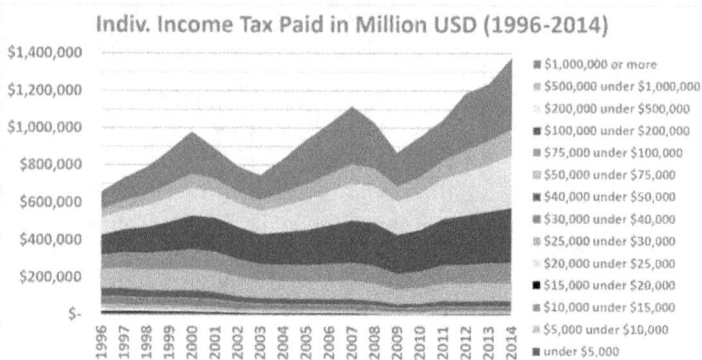

Indiv. Income Tax Paid in Million USD (1996-2014)

Source: Data from the IRS, Table 1.2 All Returns: Adjusted Gross Income, Exemptions, Deductions, and Tax Items 1996-2013, Individual Income Tax Return

Looking at the income tax revenue by percent contribution in the second chart, the burden carried by the richer has increased steadily since 1996. Contrary to what Skye often spouts, *in 2014, the top four brackets, of $100k or more in gross income, funded 80% of the total receipts*. In 1996, those same brackets only paid 50%. Lastly, looking at the third chart, income tax paid, the top four brackets own the largest contributions. Note that the two dips in revenue come directly from tax reforms from Presidents G.W. Bush and B. Obama, in responses to the recessions after Y2K-9/11 and then market crash in 2008.

The corporate picture looks similar to the individual taxpayer brackets – larger corporations pay higher effective rates, except for behemoth corps greater than $250 million that pay less... much less. In 2013, small corporations with assets of less than $500k and $1 million paid 20% and 25% tax rates, respectively, and corps between $1 million and $250 million in assets paid between 30 and 33%. Surprisingly, the highest bracket for corps paid 22.6%, which hardly seems fair from a rate point-of-view. By the way, companies with zero assets, which are on the rise with virtual companies such as Uber and Airbnb, bounced around all over the map for the last 20 years and paid a lower rate of 25% in 2013.

Figure 19: Corporate Effective Tax Rate by Assets (1996-2013)

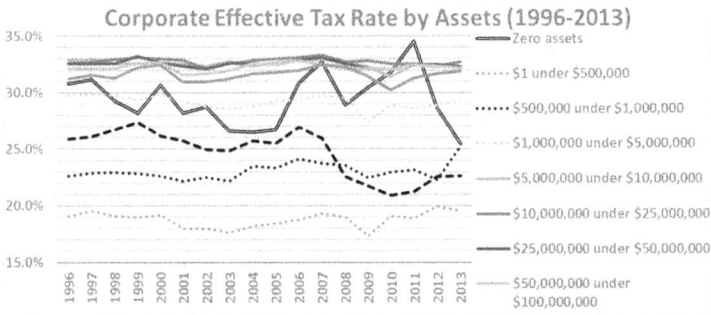

Source: Data from the IRS, Statistics of Income 1996-2013, Corporation Income Tax Return

Figure 20: Delta Effective Tax Rate Before & After Credits by Assets (1996-2013)

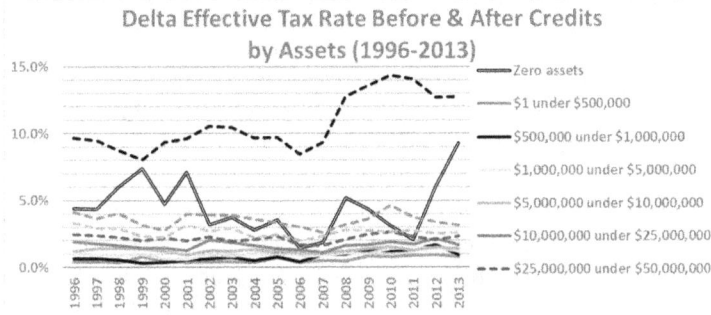

Source: Data from the IRS, Statistics of Income 1996-2013, Corporation Income Tax Return.

Figure 21: Total Corporate Income Tax Paid in Million USD (1996-2013)

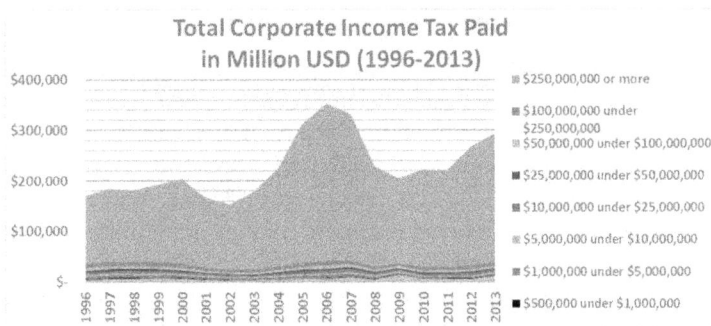

Source: Data from the IRS, Statistics of Income 1996-2013, Corporation Income Tax Return

The second chart above shows the difference in the effective tax rates before and after tax credits. Every bracket except the "zero assets" and the "greater than $250 million" had a difference of less than 5%. The zero assets corps enjoyed a 9% change while the top shelf sat at 13%. Apparently, regardless of who's in office, the government offers large breaks in the form of credit incentives to these two brackets.

Now pay close attention to the third chart. That large swath of dark matter covering just about every square inch of the graph corresponds to *the burden carried by the largest companies – an unreal 86.3% of the total corporate tax revenue*. Who said "trickle-down" is dead? The government continues to cater to mammoth corporations to keep them happy and shouldering the load.

So, back to the initial question – is corporate America carrying their weight? Consider that from 2001 to 2013, companies in the US valued at $2.5 trillion nearly doubled from 1,896 to 3,266. Even though in 2013, the top businesses paid $253 of the $293 billion collected in corporate tax revenue, that only amounted to an effective tax rate of 22.6%. Had they paid a rate similar to the rest of the midsized companies, around 32%, their contribution would have increased by around $110 billion. Considering that pre-tax profits stood at $1.9 trillion, most (especially Skye) would agree that Big Corp could and should pay more. Imagine if we were to increase the federal education budget, which totaled $154 billion in 2015, by an additional $110 billion?

And what about one-percenters – are they paying their fair share? The cut-off for the one-percent bracket sits just north of $400k gross income, which means that they shouldered about 50% of the tax load for individuals in 2013 while paying the highest effective rate at 31.6%. Unlike big corps, one-percenters do pay their share.

Now, could the top individuals and corporations pay more than ~33% in taxes? In the past, the federal government has taxed the bejeezus out of the top earners. During WWI, the highest tax bracket rates increased temporarily to 50% and then from WWII through the Korean War, the tax rate peaked at 90% as the government struggled to bring in revenue from any source possible (the actual effective tax rate landed near 50%, which still reigns substantial). However, in today's world, that could turn into a losing proposition quickly as wealthy millionaires and billionaires would pick up their toys and leave to more tax-friendly countries. There is a delicate balance between taxing them enough to pay their share and over-taxing them so much that they exit stage left.

(ASIDE: The idea that raising taxes would increase government revenue, or vice versa, vastly oversimplifies the relationship between cause and effect. In reality, there exist three components to the overall production equation: consumption, investment, and government spending. For example, when the government spending went through the roof during WWII, the GDP grew accordingly, pulling the US out of The Great Depression. Similarly, during the 1990s, a rise in investment drove up consumption which directly increased production. Lowering taxes effectively increases consumption and, thereby, investments, which was the crux behind "trickle-down" economics, at least per Tanner and his R. Reagan-loving friends and we will have more on that subject later.)

Revenue changes over time

The breakdown of sources of revenue has not remained static over time. Looking at the history of federal income since the 1930's, when the White House Office of Management and Budget began publishing it broken down by category, we can see how the receipts have changed radically as a percentage of the total revenue.

Figure 22: Sources of Federal Revenue – 1934

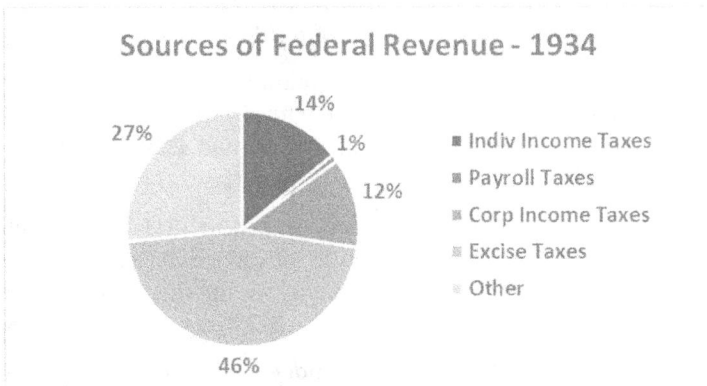

Source: Data from the White House Office of Management and Budget, Table 2.1 – Receipts by Source 1934-2021

In 1934, individuals and corporations contributed equally in the mid-teens whereas the payroll tax, instituted two years before the New Deal from Franklin Delano Roosevelt (FDR), stood as a minuscule portion of the receipts. Nearly 70% of the revenue at that time came from excise and other taxes.

Figure 23: Sources of Federal Income in Percent (1935-2015)

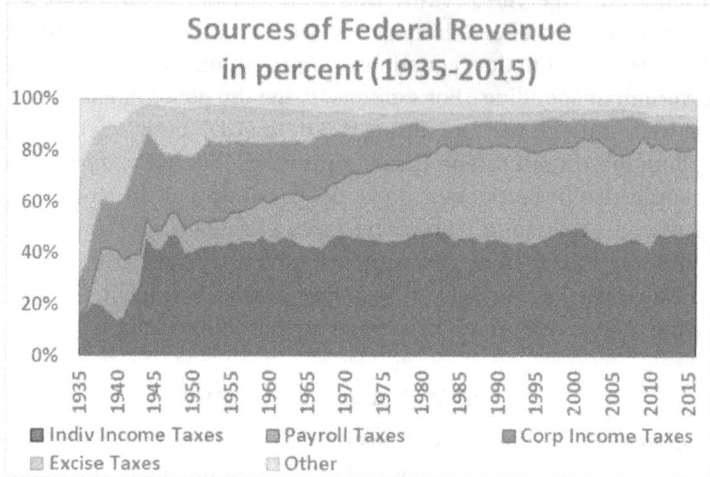

Source: Data from the White House Office of Management and Budget, Table 2.1 – Receipts by Source 1934-2021

After the Crash of 1929 and into the early 1930s, the government was in dire need of revenue to fund the federal programs started by H. Hoover and then by FDR's New Deal. Here we summarized the sources of income changes from 1934 to 2015:

- The individual income tax contribution, as a percentage of the overall revenue, climbed quickly from the mid-10% at the onset of the 1930s and into the mid-40% during WWII, where it has remained firmly for the last 70 years.

- The corporate income tax peaked in 1943 at 40% then decayed steadily to around 10% since the 1980s, as the government began to increase the contributions of individual taxpayers slowly.

- The payroll tax, which did not exist before The Great Depression, peaked briefly in the mid-20% during WWII, retreated into the single digits briefly during the 1950s then grew steadily back to the high-30% range, where it has stayed since the 1980s.

- The excise tax peaked at 46% in 1934 as the feds taxed just about every consumable, including electricity, during The Great Depression. The rate dropped quickly, though, dipping below 20% by the mid-1940s then continued to decline steadily, dropping below 5% in the 1980s, where it plateaued.

- The "other" bucket also received a temporary influx of funds in the form of estate and gift taxes in the 1930s and 1940s. However, that flow of funds shrunk significantly from a peak of 60 percent of receipts collected in 1948 to about 10 percent today.

However, the breakdown of contribution by percentage does not paint the entire picture. We need to focus also on the more than 1,000 times growth of the federal budget since the 1930s – from nearly $3 billion to over $3 trillion in 2015. Also, from the next chart, we can ascertain when significant tax reforms took effect and their effect on the Federal revenue stream. Reactionary in nature, most of these changes in the receipts slope coincide with new administrations taking over and promising tax restructuring.

Figure 24: Sources of Federal Revenue in Million USD (1935-2015)

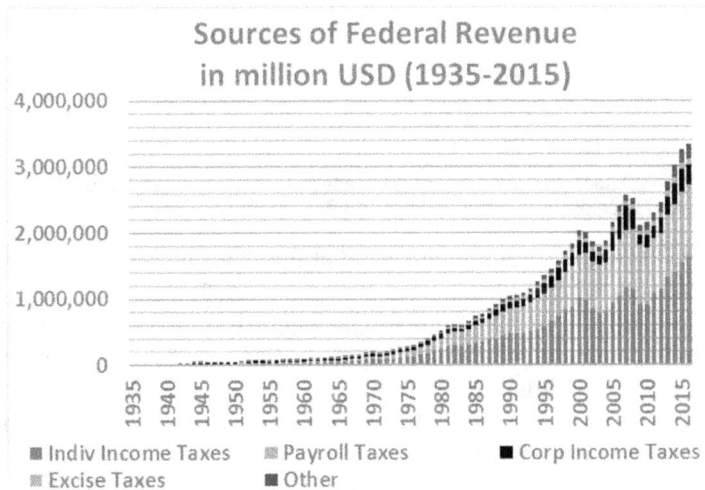

Source: Data from the White House Office of Management and Budget, Table 2.1 – Receipts by Source 1934-2021

R. Reagan's massive tax reform in 1981, then again in 1986, shuffled the receipts and briefly flattened the influx of revenue. Two terms later, facing a reduction in revenues, Bush Sr. raised the tax burden on Americans especially the high earners, which ended up costing him the 1992 elections but paved the way for the coming economic boom. Not wanting to rock the boat, B. Clinton rode the Bush Sr. tax wave right into Y2K along with increased revenues from the tech bubble. The tax reforms of Bush Jr in 2001, then B. Obama in 2009, offered temporary relief to taxpayers, but quickly returned to their previous levels when the realization settled in of the exponential growth of outlays from the War on Terror and then The Great Recession.

Figure 25: Federal Revenue vs. Budget & Spending in Trillion USD (1970-2015)

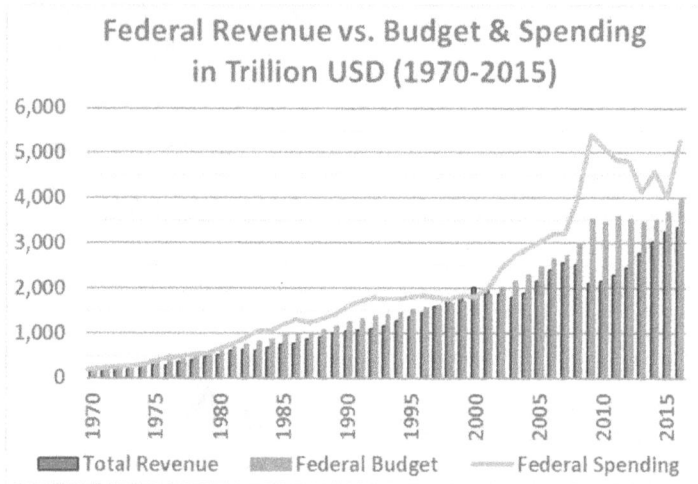

Federal Revenue vs. Budget & Spending in Trillion USD (1970-2015)

Source: Data from the White House Office of Management and Budget, Federal Receipts vs. Budget and Spending, 1970-2021

Had revenue collection remained at the pre-2000 slope, the debt would sit below $10 trillion at the end of 2015. However, raising taxes has proven a very unpopular political move, so most new administrations favor to kick off their time in office by lowering them. Bush Jr's lower taxes came on the heels of the temporary post-Y2K recession while B. Obama's hands were forced by the Great Recession of 2008.

The previous chart displays the revenue collected by the federal government vs. the planned budget and the actual spend from 1970-2015. In one chart, this diagram shows the problem and why the debt keeps growing – the revenue has not kept up with the budget, much less the spending.

So, where is all this government spending going anyways?

Chapter 4

Federal spending

TANNER VS. SKYE: In addition to many of his other self-appointed civic duties on social media, one of Tanner's favorite pastimes involves pointing out overt governmental overspending in Washington. A particularly favored meme of Tanner, which he has reposted several times over the years, is one stating the annual salaries of the president and several senior members of the White House and Congress stamped with "FOR LIFE" after each with the clincher: "I think we found where to start the cuts!"

Skye, on the other hand, does not seem too concerned with salaries in DC. She has bigger fish to fry. She prefers to focus on the long laundry list of gross negligent waste pointed out by her Democratic-Socialist fiscal champion, Bernie Sanders. If Skye had her druthers, regardless of political party affiliations, the next president should appoint Bernie as the head of the Treasury Department. He would whip those shameless over-spenders into tip-top shape in no time.

Governmental wasteful spending seems to be the one common ground between Tanner and Skye, although, where to cut would consume them. Skye has called for our government to stop the insane levels of military spending while Tanner keeps banging on the Obamacare and "welfare handouts" drum.

Figure 26: Meme entries from Tanner and Skye on wasteful government spending

GOVERNMENT WASTE

WAGES

- Salary of US President $450,000 FOR LIFE
- Salary of US Vice-President $225,000 FOR LIFE
- Salary of Speaker of the House $223,500 FOR LIFE
- Salary of the Majority Senate Leader $193,400 FOR LIFE
- Salary of the Minority Senate Leader $193,400 FOR LIFE
- Salary of House/Senate Members $174,000 FOR LIFE

I THINK WE FOUND WHERE TO START THE CUTS!

WASTEFUL GOV'T PROGRAMS

Annual Savings from program elimination

1. Eliminate the Rural Utilities Service $9.6 billion
2. Eliminate Community Dev Block Grants $3.0 billion
3. Reduce Medicare Improper Payments 50% $4.3 billion
4. Eliminate the Sugar Subsidy $1.2 billion
5. Sell the Southeastern Power Administration $1.2 billion
6. Eliminate the Dairy Subsidy $1.1 billion

These programs were identified by multiple watchdog programs to add little value for cost to operate

Source: Adapted from popular social media memes

THE REAL STORY: For the 2015 fiscal year, Congress approved the $3.7 trillion budget submitted by the White House. The federal budget consolidates over 4,000 line items into ten basic categories:

Health Care, Pensions, Defense, Welfare, Education, Transportation, General Government, Protection, Other, and Interest.

The chart below shows the breakdown of the budget by these ten high-level categories. In 2015, we overspent this budget by $438.4 billion, which when compared to the $1.1 trillion overage from the previous year seems like a bargain.

Figure 27: Government Spending in Billion USD – 2015

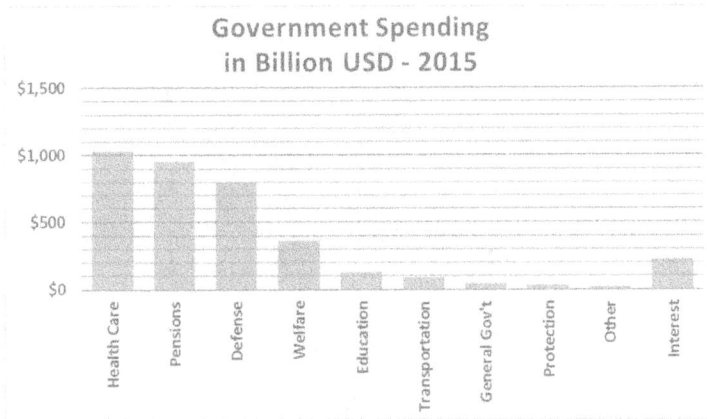

Source: Data from the White House Office of Management and Budget, Table 3.2 – Outlays by Function and Sub-Function

Types of spending

The federal government has two types of spending: mandatory and discretionary. The mandatory bucket, which accounts for about two-thirds of the overall budget in 2015, $2.52 trillion, includes mostly entitlement items such as Social Security, Medicare, Medicaid and food stamps (now known as the Supplemental Nutrition Assistance Program, SNAP). Note that the government designates Social Security as an entitlement item, even though the programs gets its funding directly from worker's contributions. In reality, the workers are just reclaiming the money they put into the fund, so technically it should not count as an entitlement item.

Figure 28: Federal Spending – Mandatory in Million USD – 2015

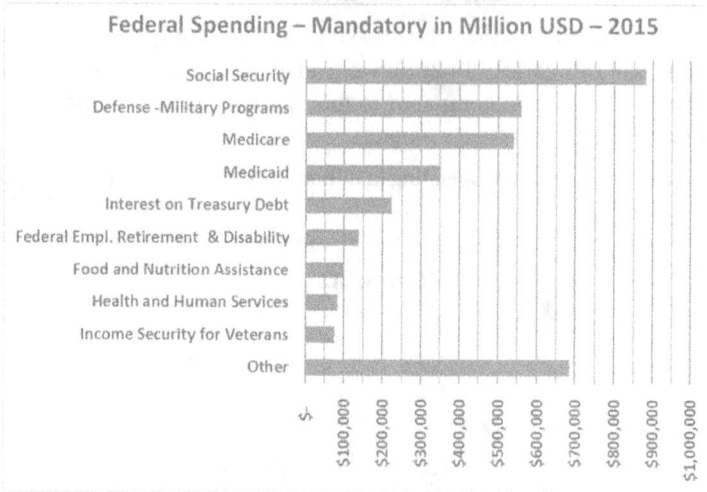

Federal Spending – Mandatory in Million USD – 2015

Source: Data from the White House Office of Management and Budget,
Table 8.1 – Outlays for Mandatory and Related Programs

Congress dictates the spending of mandatory programs outside of
the annual legislative cycle. For example, the money paid to Social
Security recipients depends on the conditions set for eligibility and
benefit level, i.e., the retiree's age and amount contributed. Congress establishes these criteria periodically, as opposed to every
year as part of the annual fiscal budget negotiations. Social
Security, Medicare, and Medicaid accounted for over 70% of the
mandatory spending in 2015. Interest paid on the debt also counts
against the mandatory spending. In the chart below, debt interest
rated as the fourth largest outlay, at $223.2 billion.

Figure 29: Federal Spending – Discretionary in Million USD – 2015

Federal Spending - Discretionary in million USD - 2015

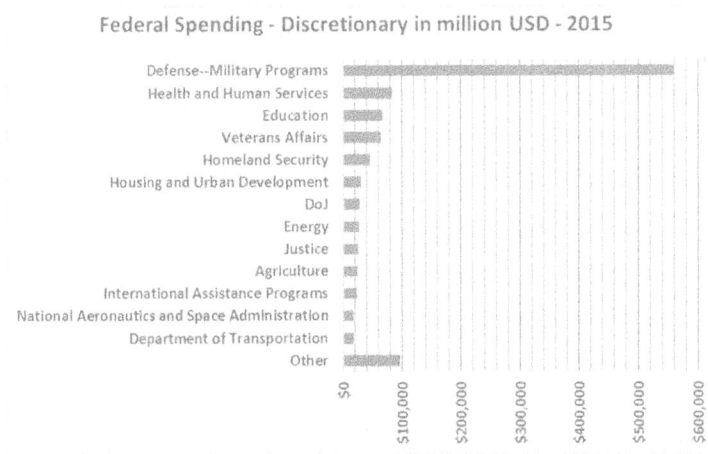

Source: Data from the White House Office of Management and Budget, Table 5.4 – Discretionary Budget Authority by Agency

The discretionary spending bucket refers to the portion of the budget negotiated annually in the context of the appropriation process, which accounted for $1.12 trillion in 2015. Half of this spending ($560.4 billion) goes to the military. Health and Human Services, Education, Veterans Affairs, and Homeland Security accounted for another 30% of the spending. Programs that get lost in the shuffle receiving the remaining 20% include important social programs such as Housing & Urban Development and Transportation along with much-needed areas of future technological growth, Energy, NASA and the National Science Foundation. International Assistance Programs also fall in the last 20%, which added to nearly $24 billion for global humanitarian aid, human rights, health, education, environment and peace & security.

The CBO and OMB started to publish the parsed mandatory vs. discretionary data in 1962. If we plot the spending by these categories since then, we can see how the overall budget aggressively grew from a little over $100 billion to nearly $4 trillion, and how the percentage flipped to the mandatory side receiving the lion's share since the 1990s.

Figure 30: Mandatory vs. Discretionary Spending in Billion USD (1962-2015)

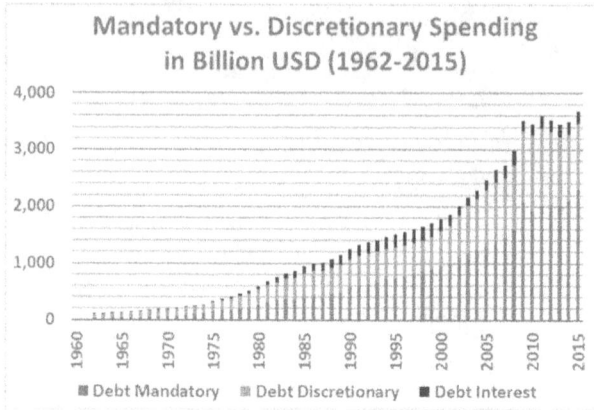

Source: Data from the White House Office of Management and Budget,
Table 8.1 – Outlays by Budget Enforcement Act Category

In 1962, we spent 67.5% of the budget on discretionary items,
while in 2015, mandatory spending accounted for 62.3% of the
annual budget. The interest on the debt had remained surprisingly
flat, hovering in the single digits, except for the R. Reagan and
G.W.H. Bush terms when it pushed into the mid-teens, during the
high-interest rates era after The Great Inflation period. However,
there is a lot more to that story, and we will cover that a little later in
the "Debt Interest & Impending Doom" chapter.

Figure 31: Mandatory vs. Discretionary Spending Percentage (1962-2015)

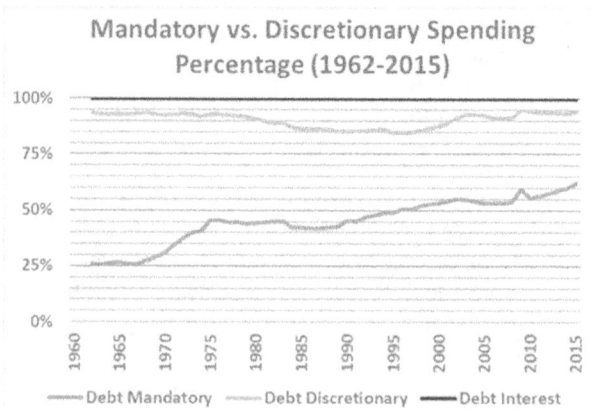

Source: Data from the White House Office of Management and Budget,
Table 8.1 – Outlays by Budget Enforcement Act Category

Spending changes over time

When we analyze the spending going back to the turn of the 20th century, in terms of percentage of the total budget, we find a few interesting nuggets.

Figure 32: Federal Spending by Area in Billion USD (1900-2015)

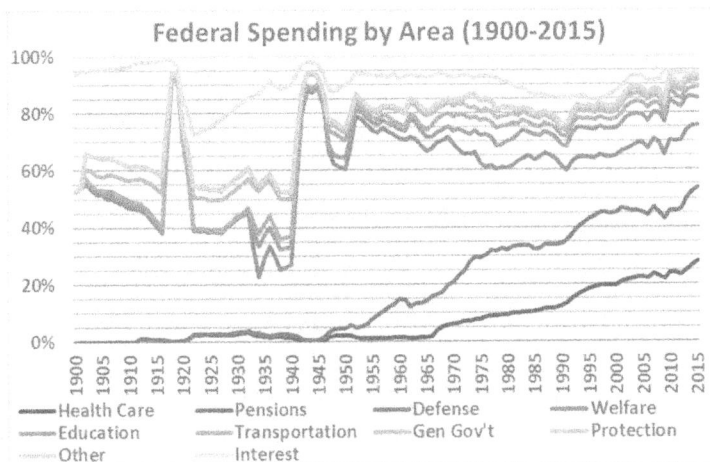

Source: Data from the White House Office of Management and Budget, Table 3.2 – Outlays by Function and Sub-Function

- As expected, military spending peaked during WWI and WWII at a ginormous ~90% of the budget.

- Contrary to what Skye would swear, military spending has continued to drop since the Second World War: from 70% in the 1950s, to 50% in the 1960s, to 30% by the 1970s, then settled at just south of 20% of the budget since the Bush Sr's last two years in office.

- R. Reagan did increase the dollars spent on defense, but since the overall budget has continued to grow, this hawk essentially maintained the military spend at ~25%, surprisingly at the same level as his uber-dove predecessor, J. Carter.

- Social programs in the Health Care, Pensions, and Welfare categories did not exist before FDR but now compose nearly two-thirds of the federal budget.

- The "Other" bucket, which constituted about 40% of spending in 1900, has gradually sunk into the single digits and to less than 1% by recent count.

- The cost to run the government has remained steady at 1% of the budget since 2000, which in 2015 translated to a little over $40 billion dollars.

So far we have covered how the government makes money and how they have overspent it, leading to a $20 trillion debt. So, with all the money we keep borrowing – who holds the debt? Is China buying the US one Silicon Valley house at a time?

Chapter 5

Who owns the debt?

First, let's start with the how, i.e., the types of Treasury Securities that the federal government uses to borrow money. The "marketable" debt, traded in secondary markets, includes Treasury bills, notes, bonds, and Treasury Inflation-Protected Securities (TIPS). The "nonmarketable" debt comprises U.S. savings securities, Government Account Series (GAS), and State and Local Government Series (SLGS).

Figure 33: Types of Treasury Securities Outstanding in Billion USD -2015

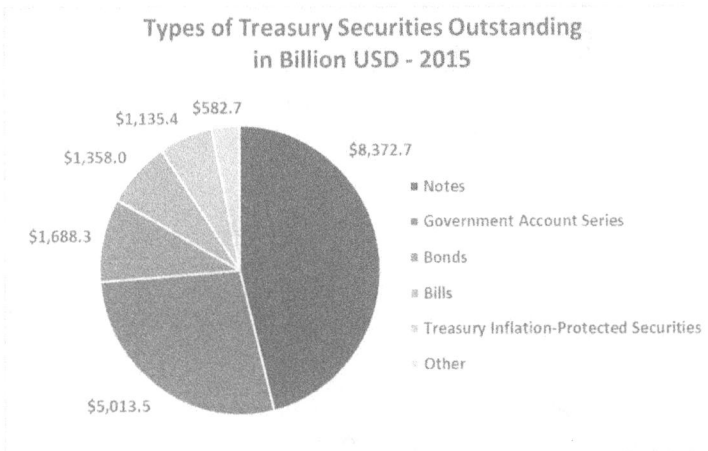

Types of Treasury Securities Outstanding
in Billion USD - 2015

$582.7
$1,135.4
$1,358.0
$8,372.7
$1,688.3
$5,013.5

- Notes
- Government Account Series
- Bonds
- Bills
- Treasury Inflation-Protected Securities
- Other

Source: Data from the Department of the Treasury, Monthly Statement of the Monthly Debt at the end of Fiscal Year 2015

The GAS covers the special securities issued to borrow from government trust funds, such as the Social Security Trust Fund, the Federal Employee Retirement Funds, the Unemployment Trust Fund, etc. *In other words, the ones used to raid our countries 401k accounts, pensions, and safety nets.* Security notes accounted for nearly half (46.1%) of the instruments. The GAS slush funds accounted for 27.7% while bonds, bills, TIPS, and other justified the last 26.2%.

Now let's discuss the who. At the end 2015, three-quarters of the national debt came from three sources:

- Foreign and International sources - 33.6% or $6.1 trillion

- Intra-Governmental Holdings - 27.7% or $5.0 trillion

- System Open Market Accounts (SOMA) managed by the Federal Reserve - 13.6% or $2.5 trillion

Figure 34: Who Owns the $18.2 Trillion Debt? In Billion USD – 2015

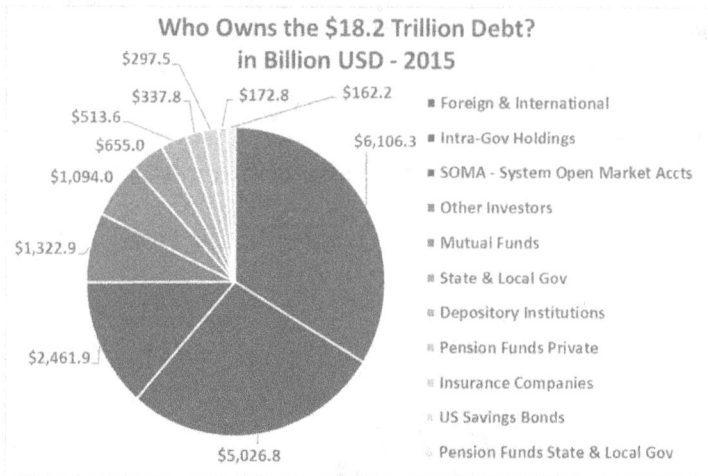

Who Owns the $18.2 Trillion Debt? in Billion USD - 2015

- Foreign & International — $6,106.3
- Intra-Gov Holdings — $5,026.8
- SOMA - System Open Market Accts — $2,461.9
- Other Investors — $1,322.9
- Mutual Funds — $1,094.0
- State & Local Gov — $655.0
- Depository Institutions — $513.6
- Pension Funds Private — $337.8
- Insurance Companies — $297.5
- US Savings Bonds — $172.8
- Pension Funds State & Local Gov — $162.2

Source: Data from the Office of Debt Management, Office of the Under Secretary for Domestic Finance, Table OFS-2—Estimated Ownership of U.S. Treasury Securities

Of the Foreign & International Holders of our debt, China and Japan owned the biggest slices of the pie at 20.6% and 19.3%. Brazil led the rest of the countries at 4.1%, followed by a host of nations in the 3-4% range – Switzerland, Cayman Islands, Ireland, United Kingdom, Hong Kong, and Luxembourg. Arab countries, Saudi Arabia and the United Arab Emirates, owned a combined 3% of our debt.

Figure 35: Foreign Holders of Treasury Securities in Million USD – 2015

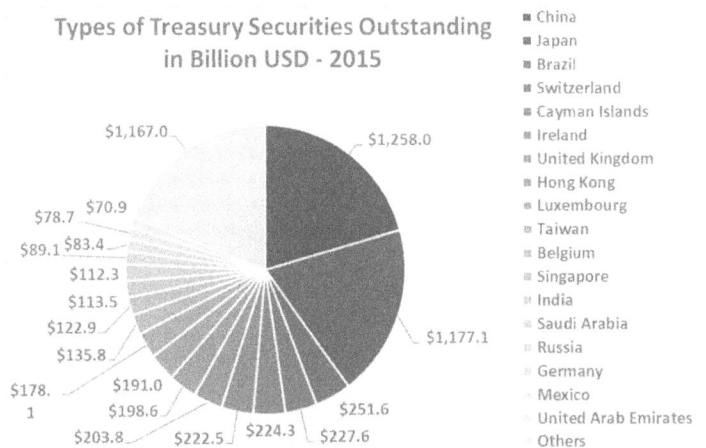

Types of Treasury Securities Outstanding in Billion USD - 2015

$1,167.0
$1,258.0
$78.7 $70.9
$89.1 $83.4
$112.3
$113.5
$122.9
$135.8
$178.1
$191.0
$198.6
$251.6
$1,177.1
$203.8 $222.5 $224.3 $227.6

■ China
■ Japan
■ Brazil
■ Switzerland
■ Cayman Islands
■ Ireland
■ United Kingdom
■ Hong Kong
■ Luxembourg
■ Taiwan
■ Belgium
■ Singapore
■ India
■ Saudi Arabia
■ Russia
■ Germany
■ Mexico
■ United Arab Emirates
■ Others

Source: Data from the Department of the Treasury, Federal Reserve Board, Major Foreign Holders of Treasury Securities

Therefore, from a total viewpoint, China and Japan own a sizeable 6.9% and 6.5% of the US debt, respectively. However, the sobering takeaway from this exercise, in addition to the exorbitant size of the debt, is *how much we keep "borrowing" from existing Intra-Government Holdings, i.e., Social Security and other funds, which now account for 27.7% of the debt!*

Going back to the credit card analogy, imagine if the Barleycorns paid a portion of their monthly credit card bills with borrowed funds from their 401k. Borrowing money from their retirement account stands as a lose-lose scenario for Jonathan and Maria. Not only is the money they borrowed not working for them by earning them compounded interest rate, rather, the money is working against them because they are paying interest on the loaned amount. At some point, if Jonathan and Maria continue to tap their nest egg, they will effectively exhaust their pensions and retirement accounts to the point that they will not be able to sustain their re-tired financial obligations. The Barleycorns are learning the hard way that borrowing from their retirement accounts is an unsustain-able losing proposition; that it is not free money.

Chapter 6

Gross Domestic Product & debt

So far, we have discussed the federal budget and national debt in detail, but to frame their size, we need to reference them relative to the Gross Domestic Product, GDP, of the United States. The GDP consists of all the goods, products, and services sold in the country, not including overseas investments by its residents or income earned by non-residents. In the Barleycorn family analogy, their "national debt" amounts to the money they owe to their creditors – their mortgage, car loans, and credit card balances. Their annual household income, salaries & investments, then represent their equivalent of the GDP.

Figure 36: US Gross Domestic Product (1790-2015)

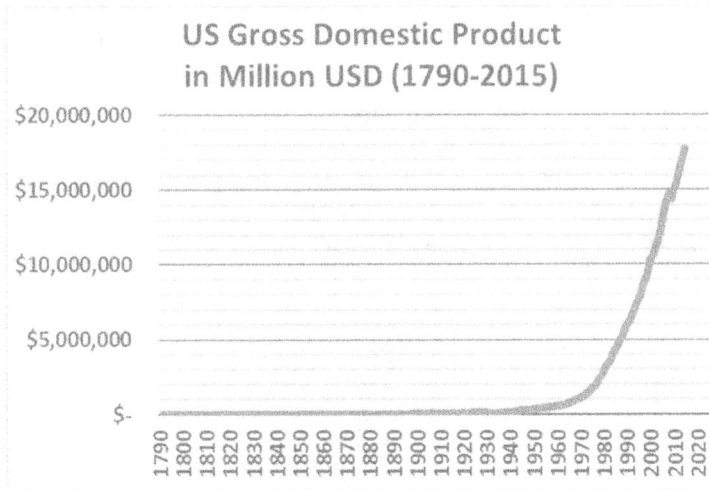

Source: Data from the White House Office of Management and Budget, Table 1.2 – Summary of Receipts, Outlays, and Surpluses or Deficits as Percentages of GDP

The previous chart plots the GDP by nominal value, which graphically starts to rise in 1950 then takes off like an Apollo rocket in 1970. It is pretty much a useless chart other than to surmise that the GDP is growing very rapidly.

Figure 37: Nominal vs. Actual GDP in Million 2015 USD (1790-2015)

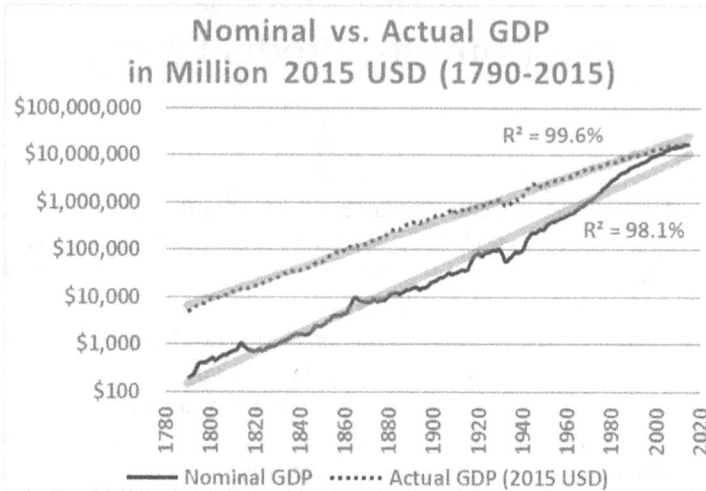

Source: Data from the White House Office of Management and Budget,
Table 1.2 – Summary of Receipts, Outlays, and Surpluses or Deficits as
Percentages of GDP

Now, in this chart, we re-plotted the same data using a log scale
that shows how the GDP rises exponentially over time (linear on the
log scale), starting at $200 million, and now sitting at nearly $20
trillion. We also added an "inflation-corrected" GDP for reference
using 2015 US dollars. In this chart, we can readily identify when
we reached certain milestones that disappear in the noise of the
first graph. The GDP started at ~$200 million in 1790. We crossed
the $1 billion threshold by 1830, $10 billion by 1880, $100 billion by
1930, $1 trillion by 1970, and $10 trillion in 2000. The GDP curve
accelerated a bit as Y2K neared but has slowed down as of late,
bringing it back towards the trend line (which by the way has a
ridiculously good 98.1% R-Squared value for correlation, meaning
that the predictive trend line matches the data extremely well). At
this rate, we will cross the $100 trillion and, gasp, the $1 quadrillion
GDP milestones in this century. For reference, the "inflation-
corrected" curve has an even higher correlation factor at 99.6%.
This highly correlated inflation-corrected trend will come in very
handy later when we break down the performance of presidents
over time.

Figure 38: Federal Spending to GDP Percentage (1790-2015).

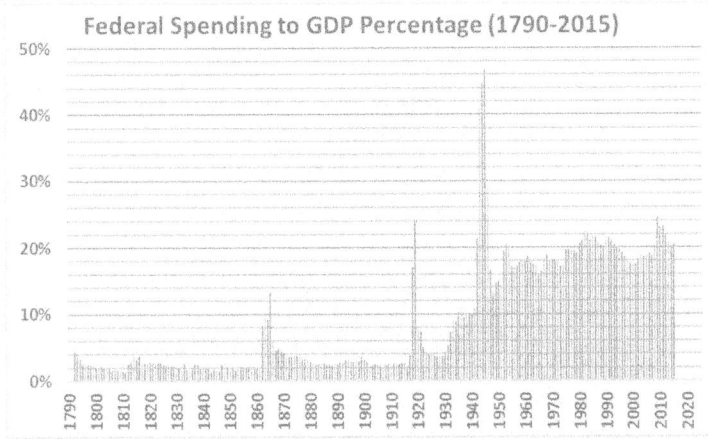

Federal Spending to GDP Percentage (1790-2015)

Source: Data from the White House Office of Management and Budget, Table 1.2 – Summary of Receipts, Outlays, and Surpluses or Deficits as Percentages of GDP.

The previous chart shows the size of federal spending as a percentage of the GDP. Excluding the massive peaks of the Civil War and WWI, spending remained below 4% of the GDP until The Great Depression. Disregarding the peak for WWII, the social programs instituted by FDR raised the bar on spending, steadily increasing the budget percentage of the GDP into the ~20% range. We first crossed that threshold in the 1950s and more or less remained in that ballpark.

Compared to the rest of the world, which by the last count includes about 196 countries, depending on who's counting, the US still holds the largest economy measured by GDP. Per The World Bank, the GDP of all the countries in the world accrued to $73.4 trillion in 2015 with the US accounting for $17.9 trillion, or 24.4% of the global economy (The World Bank, 2016). China, Japan, and Germany followed the US and together these four countries held half of the world's GDP.

Figure 39: GDP by Nation in Million USD – 2015

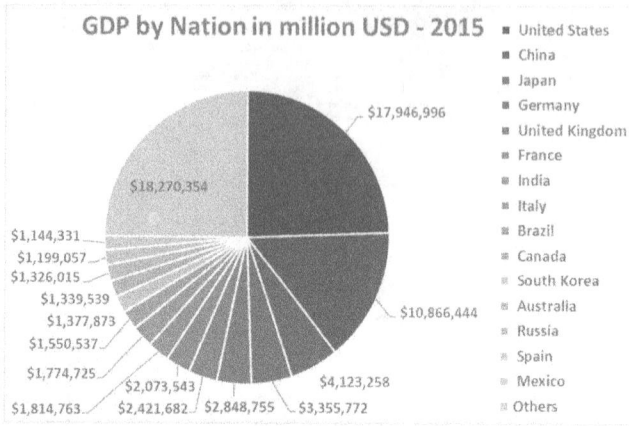

Source: Data from the World Bank, GDP Ranking Table, 2015

The previous chart shows the 15 countries that hold 75% of the world's wealth (GDP). Note that the 28-country European Union (EU), before the Brexit mess, held a combined $18.4 trillion GDP, or 25.1% of the world's economy. Less the Brits, the EU portion drops slightly to $15.6 trillion, or 21.3%. By the way, the UK already ranked as the fifth highest GDP in the world on their own – so, they will be OK, regardless of the onset of panic and fear as they ripped off the EU Band-Aid.

Figure 40: Public Debt by Nation in Million USD – 2015

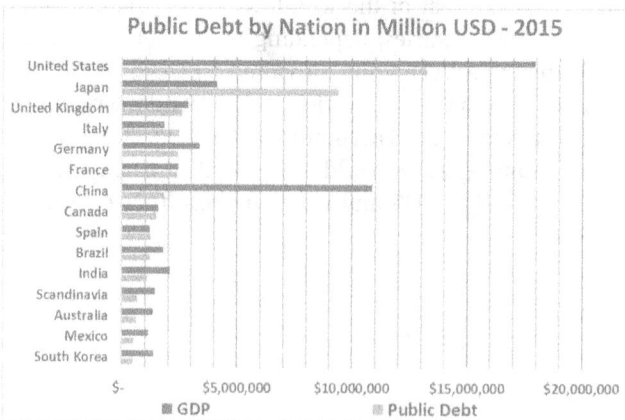

Source: Data from the Central Intelligence Agency, Library Publications, World - Public Debt by nation as percent of GDP

To give a sense of the scale of the US debt as compared to the rest of the world, above we show a chart of the public debt of the Top-15 countries by GDP. We presented the public debt instead of the total national debt (excluded the IGH portion) for two reasons. First, when comparing to other nations, we care about money owed to other countries, so we should not include debt owed to itself. Second, this difficult to find data seemed the most complete and most recent as of 2015. Interestingly enough, it came from the Central Intelligence Agency, of all places. Who da thunk that the CIA would publish such an interesting website with a library chock full of goodies? But we digress.

Anyways, the US has the largest public debt (the light gray bars in the chart above) followed by Japan, who is upside down by more than a factor of two relative to their GDP. In the Top-10 GDP countries, only Japan and Italy hold more debt than their GDP total at 225% and 135%, respectively. The countries with the least debt in the GDP Top-10, you ask? India and Brazil, who came in at 51.7% and 67.3%. We will skip China, even though on paper, it appears like China has exceedingly low debt by percent to GDP at 16.7%. Their accounting practices do not compare well to non-communist open-system economies, due to their convoluted cross-holdings classification of provincial debt, central government debt, and other shenanigans.

In summary, in 2015, the public debt of the US stood at 73.6% of its GDP. The rest of the Top-20 countries that generated 80% of the global GDP also had an aggregate debt of 72.0%. By that measurement, the US does not sit too far out of whack. However, the main problem with that comparison is that the debt is not static. Our public debt keeps mounting at an alarming pace that will grow past 100% of the GDP inside of three years. Lest we forget that we also owe another $5 trillion to IGH, which combined with the public debt already exceeded the GDP in 2015. Other countries do not have the internal resources to lend themselves trillions of dollars. So, the risk of a runaway US debt looms as a threat not just to the US, but also to the world's economy. We will detail more about this danger in the chapter on the Debt Interest.

Oh yeah, and those pesky Scandinavians only owe 46.5% of their GDP. Perhaps the Barleycorns should move there and enjoy their 35-hr work weeks, month-long vacations, free education, free healthcare, exceedingly attractive women, and endless northern lights. But, if you think Jonathan complains too much now about how Uncle Sam takes 25% of his hard-earned money, wait until he finds out that the Scandinavians dish out 60% effective tax rates to pay for all this "free stuff." One thing is for sure, though, Bernie would love it there so here's a better idea. Let's set-up Vermont as full-time Democratic-Socialist state and see how that works out for a few years before we jump on the Sander's Train.

As we unraveled the budgets, spending, and debt, we uncovered how social programs for healthcare, pensions, and welfare account-ed for the lion's share of the spend. Next, let's find out how the current social welfare system came into existence.

Chapter 7

Origin of the welfare
entitlement society

To understand how the current welfare system came about, we first need to discuss the background that led to The Great Depression. The Roaring 20's arrived on the heels and misery of the First World War. After a brief post-war recession, peace and prosperity fueled a decade of excess and greed, highlighted by undelineated boundaries between commercial and investment banking.

Figure 41: Dow Jones Industrial Average (1910-1960)

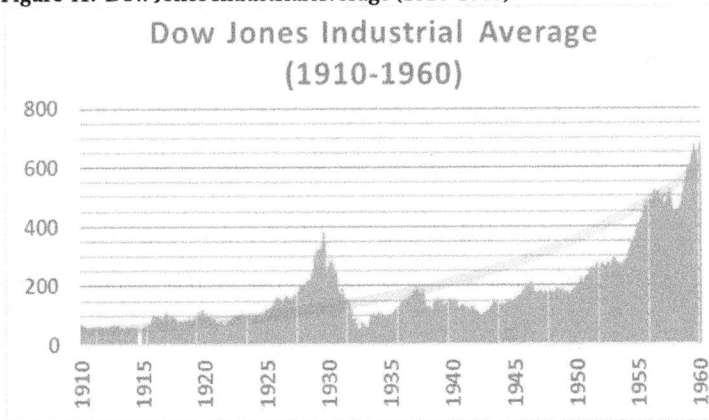

Dow Jones Industrial Average
(1910-1960)

Source: Data from Measuring Worth, Daily Closing Values of the DJA in the United States, 1885 to Present

Driven by wild speculation and financial gluttony from an unsustainable market spike (see chart above), overzealous investors and commercial banks dove head first into increasingly risky stock market investments. Eventually, the overextended banks, working without safety nets, came tumbling down, earning the bulk of the blame for the financial crisis of 1929 that kick-started The Great Depression.

From 1929 until 1931, the US suffered through a number of disastrous attempts by the H. Hoover administration to halt the slide, which included propping up wages and restricting foreign goods by the passing of the Tariff Act of 1930. Also known as the Smoot-Hawley Tariff Act, to protect American businesses and farmers, this law raised already high import duties by 20%. This Act resulted in disaster, as it not only extended the global depression but ultimately severely dampened US exports. In conjunction with some highly questionable moves by the Fed Chair, Roy Young, the economic decline accelerated. A traditionalist, Young served as Chair from 1927-1930 and preferred to focus on strengthening the banking system rather than influencing monetary policy. In an act of tough love or stupidity, he refused to bail out the banks and, worse yet, tightened the money supply. He raised the Discount Rate from 3.5% to 6% and then engaged in extensive Open Market Operations that further drained reserves from the banking system. These extremely questionable moves by the administration and Fed brought the economy to a screeching halt. Historians have speculated over the years that they turned a severe recession into a full-blown and extended depression (Sullivan, 2009). Inadvertently, H. Hoover and R. Young, essentially, put the Great in The Great Depression.

Figure 42: Inflation & Unemployment Rates in Percent (1910-1960)

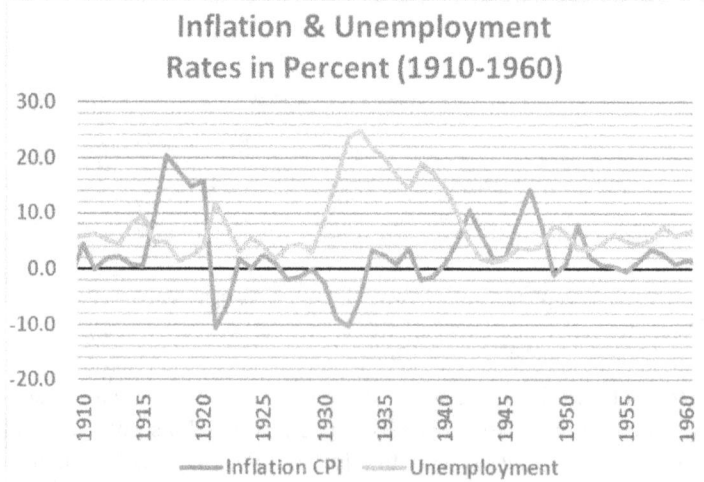

Source: Data from the Bureau of Labor and Statistics, Unemployment Rates and CPI Inflation, 1948-2015

Figure 43: US Gross Domestic Product in Million USD (1910-1960)

US Gross Domestic Product in Million USD (1910-1960)

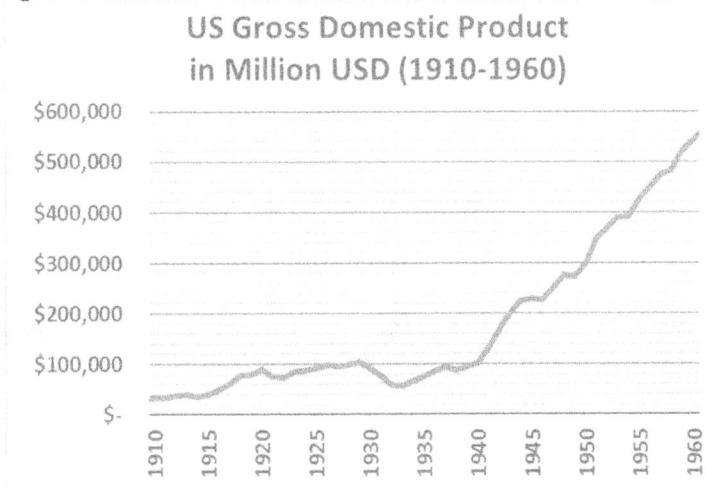

Source: Data from the White Office of Management and Budget, Table 4.1 Gross Domestic Product

With an estimated two million people homeless, a quarter of the country's workforce unemployed, and the NY Stock Exchange and GDP down to levels not seen since pre-WWI, voters, ready for change, overwhelmingly decided that the US needed to head in a new direction in the 1932 elections. They found their man in the former Assistant Secretary of the Navy and Governor of New York, F.D. Roosevelt. FDR won in a landslide, focusing his campaign on the New Deal and his motto of "Relief, Recovery, and Reform."

At this point in US history, FDR's first 100 days, the fate of our entire social and financial system changed forever, marking the beginning of the welfare entitlement society. In his first order of priority after the inauguration, FDR needed to restore America's confidence in the banking system. Without federal insurance backing their funds, the market crash caused thousands of banks to fail as billions of investment dollars vanished and citizens across the nation ran to withdraw their life savings. This only exacerbated the situation, as banks had to close because they physically ran out of money, which further fueled widespread panic. The Emergency Banking Act of 1933, enacted on day five after FDR took office, forced all banks to close temporarily while the federal government would audit them and determine which ones were deemed financially ready to resume operations. When the banks reopened a few days later, the government had propped them up with federal loans and established the Federal Deposit Insurance Corporation (FDIC) to guarantee bank deposits and, more importantly, restore consumer confidence in pulling their money out from under their mattresses and back into institutions. The Act also temporarily suspended the Gold Standard for about a year and extended unprecedented fiscal powers to the Office of the President during a time of crisis, powers which the Commander in Chief still holds today.

(ASIDE: A subsequent bill, the Banking Act of 1933, separated commercial and investment banking and became informally known as the Glass-Steagall Act. Yes, the same one that B. Clinton repealed in 1999, leading to the same type of risky investments by banks that collapsed the economy again in 2008, only this time with mortgages. We never learn, do we?)

What followed next can best be described as a commissioned free-for-all as FDR's administration tried anything and everything to get the country moving again. In all, as part of the New Deal, he and Congress formed over 100 new bureaus, offices, commissions, and administrations, in what became known as the Alphabet Agencies. Using his unprecedented fiscal powers, FDR spent more than $3 billion, a gargantuan amount in the 1930s, establishing agencies through Executive Orders in his first two years in office. While some of the agencies still exist today, the Supreme Court disbanded others, labeling them as unconstitutional. Below we highlight some of the groundbreaking Relief, Recovery, and Reform Agencies instituted by FDR.

Relief

- Federal Emergency Relief Administration: The FERA supported millions of needy households with food, clothes, and medical aid. It also funded work projects for the unemployed and provided vaccinations and literacy classes for millions of destitute folks. The Works Progress Administration (WPA) and the Social Security Act (SSA) superseded FERA in 1935, taking over in helping those in need and the unemployed. The WPA dissolved in 1943, but the Social Security Act still thrives today.

- National Youth Administration: The NYA provided useful jobs for young people across America (dissolved in 1943).

Recovery

- Federal Housing Administration: The FHA provided affordable rate loans to new homeowners for home building, which indirectly helped unemployment and the construction market. The FHA still exists today.

- Public Works Administration: The PWA, intended for both industrial recovery and unemployment relief, completed thousands of construction projects including public buildings, highways, bridges, and dams. It ended in 1938.

Reform

- Social Security Act: The SSA administered a national pension for retired persons, unemployment aid, and assistance programs for needy mothers, children, and those physically disabled. *This act became the basis for the welfare entitlement society and most the social programs still functioning today, including Social Security, Medicare, Medicaid, Unemployment, and food stamps (SNAP).*

- Securities and Exchange Commission: The SEC served as the federal "watchdog" administrative agency to protect public and private investors from Wall Street stock market fraud and insider trading. It still exists today with even more broad powers than the original Act.

- Federal Deposit Insurance Corporation: The FDIC insured bank customers against the loss of up to $5,000 of their deposits if their bank failed. The FDIC still operates insuring depositors up to $250K per insured bank.

- National Labor Relations Act: Also known as the Wagner Act of 1935, the NLRA protected the rights of labor unions to organize and collectively bargain with employers. In 1947, the Taft-Hartley Act modified the original act by restricting the activities and power of unions somewhat, but the NLRA still exists today protecting unions and laborers rights.

- Rural Electrification Administration: provided low-cost loans to farm cooperatives to bring power to their communities at a time when only 10% of farmers had access to electricity. This program thrives still via public and privately funded enterprises.

However, not all the programs succeeded. In fact, some of them set precedents still felt today:

- Civil Works Administration: The CWA employed four million people in useful and necessary construction jobs, such as repairing public works, schools, and roads. However, other jobs came under intense scrutiny and ended up characterized as wasteful, such as paying for leaf raking in the morning then leaf disbursement in the afternoon to assure the worker a job for the next day. The CWA program lasted less than a year.

- Agricultural Adjustment Act: The AAA paid farmers for not planting or burning already planted crops to reduce surpluses and increase demand for farm commodities, thereby controlling and setting crop prices. The Act helped farmers but hurt tenants and farm workers, pushing them to the unemployment lines. Also, the crop destruction became a political nightmare for FDR as millions of Americans went to bed hungry while potential crops that could feed them burned senselessly. The Supreme Court ruled the Act as unconstitutional because of lack of jurisdiction of the federal government over state matters. A second AAA in 1938 addressed the issues, and it still functions today (without the crop burning, of course).

- National Recovery Act: formed as part of the National Industrial Recovery Act, the NRA (not to be confused with the gun-happy National Rifle Association) fixed wages, business codes, and quotas artificially, in an effort to promote economic recovery. It accomplished little, and then the Supreme Court struck it down as unconstitutional.

Success or failure?

While some of FDR's Reform Agencies arrived long overdue from a social and economic point of view (labor laws, welfare for the poor, stock market protection, etc.), it ultimately failed to pull the country out of The Great Depression. In fact, in retrospect, most economists would agree that the New Deal substantially extended the depression (Sullivan, 2004). The bleak financial conditions persisted well into FDR's third term. Not until the war machinery kicked into gear, converting US factories to manufacture the necessary military arsenal and putting the country back to work, did the economy finally rebound. Unemployment peaked in 1933 at 24.9% but lingered in the 14-19% range until 1941. The Dow took two decades to return to the pre-Great Depression levels and the GDP stagnated for a decade until the attack on Pearl Harbor jump-started military production.

However, as ineffective the New Deal turned out in fixing the economy, it forced the federal budget to jump fivefold because of the newly formed social and welfare reform programs. Here to stay, *the federal budgets increased from ~4% of the GDP before The Great Depression to ~20% where they have remained since WWII.*

Figure 44: Federal Budget & Spending as Percent GDP in 2015 USD (1915-2015)

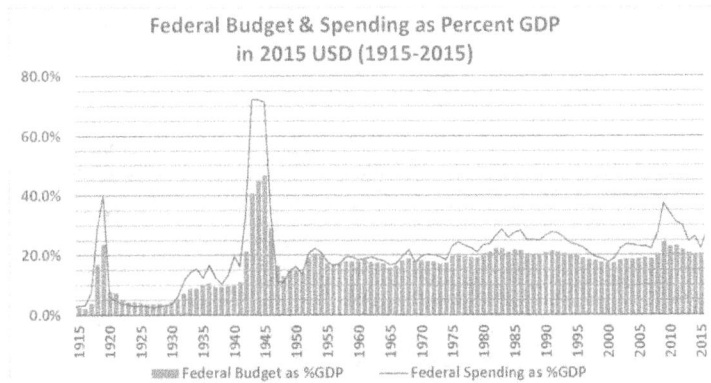

Source: Data from the White House Office of Management and Budget, Table 1.2 – Summary of Receipts, Outlays, and Surpluses or Deficits as Percentages of GDP. Conversion to 2015 USD using CPI from US Department of Labor and Statistics.

This is usually the point in the argument where Tanner would jump in to make a case for reducing social programs and government spending. Alternatively, Skye would chime in, expounding on how the money spent helps those in need, even supporting further expansion of social and welfare programs.

Understandably, F.D. Roosevelt overspent his budgets by an average of 59.2%. First, when it came to the New Deal, he preferred to err than not try at all, so he had some agency hits and some misses, which boosted his deficit ratios, especially in his first term. Then he got saddled with the most expensive war ever to date (in relation to the GDP), WWII, which catapulted the government spending into the stratosphere at 70+% of GDP.

B. Obama came the closest of any president to that level of over-spending at a modest 33.3% range in comparison. Barack, like FDR, also got dealt a crappy hand to start his administration and faced an uphill battle his entire first term, even though he managed to drop the deficit back to the levels of his predecessor by his second term.

Figure 45: Federal Budget and Spending as Percent GDP by President

President	Political Party	Federal Budget as % GDP	Federal Spending as % GDP	Overspend as % Budget	Comment
Franklin Roosevelt	Democratic	23.5%	37.3%	59.2%	The Great Depression & World War II
Barack Obama	Democratic	21.9%	29.2%	33.3%	Afghan War, Iraq War II, The Great Recession
George HW Bush	Republican	20.9%	26.7%	27.4%	Iraq War I
Ronald Reagan	Republican	21.3%	26.4%	23.6%	
George W Bush	Republican	18.8%	23.1%	22.5%	Afghanistan War & Iraq War II
Gerald Ford	Republican	19.7%	23.8%	20.5%	
Herbert Hoover	Republican	5.0%	5.7%	15.2%	Great Depression
Jimmy Carter	Democratic	19.7%	22.6%	14.5%	The Great Inflation
Bill Clinton	Democratic	18.8%	21.3%	13.1%	
Richard Nixon	Republican	17.8%	19.3%	8.4%	Vietnam War
Lyndon Johnson	Democratic	17.4%	18.8%	8.1%	Vietnam War
John Kennedy	Democratic	17.9%	19.0%	6.1%	
Dwight Eisenhower	Republican	18.1%	19.0%	4.7%	Korean War
Harry Truman	Democratic	17.3%	17.3%	-0.1%	World War II

Source: Data from the White House Office of Management and Budget, Table 1.2 – Summary of Receipts, Outlays, and Surpluses or Deficits as Percentages of GDP

Since the 1930s, only four other presidents passed the 20% threshold in deficits with respect to the budget: G.W.H. Bush (27.4%), R. Reagan (23.5%), G.W. Bush (22.5%), and G. Ford (20.5%). If we exclude the Cold War and a 10-minute military invasion of Grenada, R. Reagan stands out as the only peacetime president from the Over-Spenders Club. His massive military buildup by far drove his deficits.

Chapter 8

The Fed, gold & the debt ceiling

So, if you did not harbor adequate ill will towards Richard Milhous Nixon already, brace yourself because you might gain a couple more resentments along the way. In this section, we will discuss several topics that have deeply affected the economy of the US and particularly the debt over the last hundred years.

The Federal Reserve Bank

In the relatively short history of the United States, the federal government opened and closed a central bank twice until it stuck for good, as established by the Federal Reserve Act of 1913. Alexander Hamilton pushed for the creation of the First Bank of the US in 1781, mainly to handle the Post-War debt. When its 20-year chapter expired in 1811, the renewal fell one vote short due to a strong public opinion against a large and powerful bank. After the War of 1812, the US had once again racked up a significant amount of debt, so the Second Bank of the US came into existence. By the 1830's strong opposition to the bank, led by President Andrew Jackson this time, once again denied the charter renewal in 1836. During the Civil War, Lincoln passed the National Banking Act of 1863, which established the dollar as the official currency of the Union. The Act also provided for nationally chartered banks but stopped short of creating a central bank.

After a few waves of bank panics during the 1890s and 1900s, progressives and conservatives finally agreed on the need for a central bank, leading to the passing of the Federal Reserve Act in 1913 under Woodrow Wilson. This Act established the Federal Reserve Bank, as we know it today. Per the current mission on their website (Board of Governors of the Federal Reserve System, 2009), the responsibilities of the Federal Reserve Bank fall into four general areas:

1. To set the nation's monetary policy by influencing money and credit to lower unemployment and inflation

2. To regulate banks to ensure the safety and soundness of the nation's financial system

3. To maintain the stability of the financial system and contain systemic risk

4. To provide financial services to the U.S. government, domestic and foreign official institutions and oversee the nation's payments systems

Using these four measures as a barometer, the Fed has come up short on several occasions, most notably during The Great Depression of the 1930s, The Great Inflation of the 1970s, and the Great Recession of the 2000s. We will discuss in more detail the role of the Fed, especially as it affects monetary policy, in the next chapter on debt interest.

The Gold Standard

"We have gold because we cannot trust governments," said Herbert Hoover, who ironically presided during the market crash of 1929 and the start of The Great Depression.

The discovery of America was never about finding a shortcut to the East Indies – it was always about gold and riches. Archeologists have traced the usage of gold coins as far back as the Persian Empire in 600-700 BCE, which eventually spread to the Greek and Roman domains. Up until Europe started using paper money in the 16-17th centuries, gold coins and bullion dominated currency and trade throughout most of the civilized world. The discovery of gold in America, then later in Australia and Africa, led to the expansion of the gold coffers of European countries by several folds. By the 1800's, Europe and most of the world had established a monetary system of equivalent value between paper notes and gold – hence the Gold Standard.

The US adopted the Gold Standard in 1834 and then in 1900 passed the Gold Standard Act. This Act fixed the price of gold at $20.67/oz., where it remained until The Great Depression. In 1933, a month after taking office and in an act of desperation, FDR signed Executive Order 6102, dubbed the Great Gold Confiscation. Nearly 10,000 banks had failed in the aftermath of the market crash of 1929, causing hundreds of billions of dollars to evaporate into thin air. Many Americans literally lost all their savings overnight, since the FDIC (Federal Deposit Insurance Corporation) did not yet exist. Those with the means, however, started to hoard as much gold as they could get their hands on, taking to heart the saying "during times of war and economic uncertainty buy gold." FDR's Executive

Order forced all Americans to turn in all their gold coins, bullion, and certificates to the Federal Reserve, redeeming them for $20.67/oz in exchange for paper currency.

Historians, however, have theorized that the real reason for the gold confiscation was a bailout of the Federal Reserve Bank (Higgins, 2013). Even F.D. Roosevelt commented during one of his early "Fireside Chats" that gold obligations far exceeded the gold held by the US Treasury and Federal Reserve. After the public had turned in the majority of the gold, FDR artificially increased the price of gold to $35/oz., which, voilà, instantly bolstered the Federal Reserve holdings to support the much-needed funds to get the economy moving again. Starting in 1934, the Federal Reserve even updated the clause printed on currency bills "redeemable for gold" with "redeemable in lawful money." This innocuous act foreshadowed the abandonment of the direct exchange of the dollar to gold. But not yet. That finality would require more time, more wars, and one Milhous.

Bretton Woods and Triffin, oh my!

Toward the end of WWII with the result a foregone conclusion, delegates from forty-four Allied nations met in Bretton Woods, New Hampshire to hash out a new post-war international monetary system. The final agreement, referred to as the Bretton Woods System, consisted of all the countries locking their currencies to the US dollar, with minor adjustable controls for exceptional circumstances, and the US tying the dollar to gold, which at the time still stood at $35/oz. Another important outcome of this conference was the founding of the International Monetary Fund (IMF), whose main goals included fostering global monetary cooperation, securing financial stability and facilitating international trade. Today, 189 of 196 nations worldwide participate in the IMF organization (not to be confused with the Impossible Missions Force and the string of progressively awful movies by Tom Cruise).

However, while the IMF still functions today, the Bretton Woods System collapsed within three decades as anticipated by Belgian economist Robert Triffin and his namesake dilemma. The final straw came when the US abandoned the Gold Standard in 1971. The Triffin Dilemma, which sounds more like something out of a Harry Potter book, described the contradiction in the short-term domestic and the long-term international economic objectives of the country offering the monetary standard, the US in this case.

Ultimately, the imbalance results in an unworkable currency trade deficit that pretty much described what would happen over the next quarter century.

As speculated by Triffin, the deficit arose from the need of the country with the global standard currency, the US, to supply other countries with sufficient currency to fulfill the demand for their foreign exchange reserves. Due to the outflow of dollars in trade, and especially, from the post-war Marshall Plan to rebuild Europe, by the end of the 1950s, the US held barely enough gold reserves ($19.4 billion) to back the US currency owned by foreign countries ($18.7 billion). A decade later, the US international deficit was upside down by more than $30 billion, which ultimately started to devalue the dollar and increase the price of gold. By the 1960s, gold traded for $40/oz in the London black market, even though the artificially set price still stood at $35/oz. Towards the end of the 1960s and into the 1970s, the US got hammered with the economic triple whammy:

1. A growing international currency deficit

2. A mounting domestic fiscal deficit and recession from the Vietnam War and Johnson's social programs to abolish poverty

3. A self-induced stagflation period (stagnant economic demand combined with high inflation and high unemployment) from R. Nixon's economic policies.

So, you see where all of this is headed, right? By 1971, the US had no other choice but to abandon the Gold Standard. At the time, R. Nixon claimed the gold detachment would only be a temporary measure; that the US would re-instate it. However, time proved differently, and the global era of fixing currency to gold had come and gone. Virtually all the world's nations now use a "fiat" currency system, which means that the government backs the legal tender.

(*ASIDE*: We can argue the merits of an alternative solution to abandoning the standard: R. Nixon could have instead raised the value of gold à la FDR. Interestingly enough, this is exactly what transpired to the price of gold when allowed to float in a free market. The value of gold shot up suddenly and by the end of the 1970s, an ounce of gold sold for over $400 (the value of gold peaked in 2011 at $1,895/oz.). However, this would have proven only a short-term solution, as the US budget, debt, and deficits would climb from the billions to the trillions over the next four decades. The value of gold would have had to increase to nearly $75,000/oz by now to keep up with the US outstanding commitments of the national debt and currency in circulation. Per the Department of Treasury, at the end of 2015, the US held 261.5 million fine troy ounces of gold reserves in deep storage mints (such as Ft Knox), mint working stock (coin blanks and such) and Federal Reserve Bank vaults (such as the one in New York that Jeremy Irons robbed in Die Hard 3 with the stolen dump trucks). Even at today's price of gold, around $1,250/oz., this would only amount to a $350 billion reserve, which looks like chump change in terms of today's federal budget.)

While many believed that ending the US tie to gold spelled economic doom for the dollar and the US, not all of the news was bad for Uncle Sam. Some economists claim the counter argument that unlocking the dollar from the Gold Standard paid dividends in the 1970s and 1980s. Devaluing the dollar against other currencies made US manufacturing exports cheaper and more attractive worldwide. In fact, throughout history, the central banks of other countries have routinely suspended or abandoned the Gold Standard when deemed necessary or convenient. Case in point, the UK suspended the Gold Standard during WWI, only to re-establish it a few years later under Winston Churchill before abandoning it for good in the 1930s in preparations for WWII (Titcomb, 2015).

For a long time, while we still had a manageable debt level, locking the dollar to gold held back runaway overspending since the US, in theory, needed to maintain sufficient gold in reserves to back its obligations. As mentioned earlier, the US crossed that line in the 1950s never to look back. With no other mechanisms in place, abandoning the Gold Standard in 1971 released the last bit of virtual control on the mounting US debt, and the race to overspend was on like Donkey Kong.

Figure 46: US Surplus/Deficits – Public vs. IGH in Million USD (1950-2015)

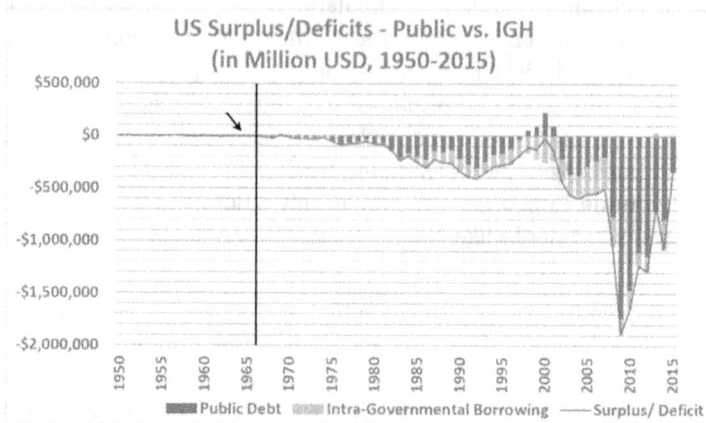

Source: Data from the White House Office of Management and Budget, Table 7.1 - Federal Debt at the End of the Year 1940-2021

Figure 47: US Surplus/Deficits to GPD Percentage (1950-2015)

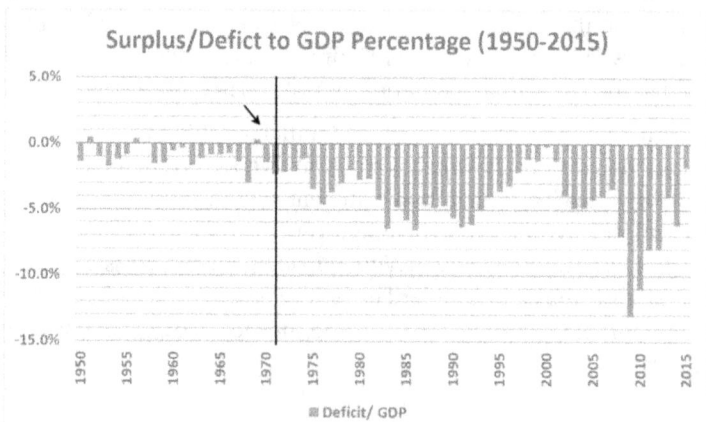

Source: Data from the White House Office of Management and Budget, Table 7.1 - Federal Debt at the End of the Year 1940-2021

The arrows in the previous charts highlight the last federal surplus of $2.9 billion in 1969, then show how the overspending exploded after R. Nixon abandoned the Gold Standard in 1971. Save for the tech bubble temporarily correcting the annual deficits in the 1990s, the percent spent systematically increased from an average of ~2% pre-1970 to ~5% of the GDP since the mid-1970s. After peaking at an unreal 13% in 2009, due to the Wall Street Bailout, the last seven years under the B. Obama administration show an aggressive trend to lower the deficit. However, after a promising 2015, it appears that 2016 will land back to the ~5% average.

What about the debt ceiling, isn't that supposed to limit the spending? Yeah... no, which leads us to the next topic.

The Debt Ceiling

Remember that fiasco at the end of 2015 when the government was about to shut down, closing the National Park System and threatening to send additional hordes of federal employees home on furloughs because we were about to run out of money? Well, the debt ceiling caused that fiasco. To understand the debt ceiling, let's first break down how the budget process works at a high level.

When Warren Harding signed the Budget and Accounting Act of 1921, he founded two offices that still function today – the Office of Management and Budget (OMB) and the Government Accountability Office (GAO). Originally reporting to the Treasury Department and called the Bureau of the Budget, the OMB moved under the legislative branch in 1939 to stay. The main purpose of the OMB remains to help the president prepare the annual federal budget to send to Congress for approval, while the non-partisan GAO audits and reports on all matters of public funding and spending, making recommendations on where to improve economies of scale and efficiencies.

In the midst of the Watergate scandal, and well-deserved distrust of the legislative branch, Congress passed the Congressional Budget Act of 1974, which created the Congressional Budget Office (CBO) and added another level of bureaucracy and negotiations to the budget approval process. The OMB would send the proposed budget to the CBO, who in turn scrutinized it and proposed its final version for approval by the House and Senate. In summary, the budget approval process entails a five-step procedure:

Step 1: The President and the OMB prepare an annual budget and submit it to Congress

Step 2: The nonpartisan CBO helps the House and Senate analyze and pass budget resolutions

Step 3: The Appropriations Committee for each house of Congress finalize the bills

Step 4: The House and Senate vote on the bills

Step 5: The President signs the bills into law

In theory, the budgetary process should stop at those first five steps. However, what happens if we go over the budget, which has occurred every year since 1969? This is where the debt ceiling comes into play.

The ceiling story began in 1917 when the US started to accumulate unprecedented debt due to WWI. The need to raise money for the War forced Congress to pass the Second Liberty Bond Act, which indirectly established the debt ceiling. The act allowed the US Treasury to issue certain bond debt instruments for specific purposes up to a limit. After a lull during the 1920s, the debt ceiling began to climb in earnest during The Great Depression then jumped into hyper-drive throughout WWII. After the war, the ceiling stayed mostly in check until the 1970s when it began to climb at a rapid pace.

Figure 48: Debt Ceiling in Billion USD (1960-2015)

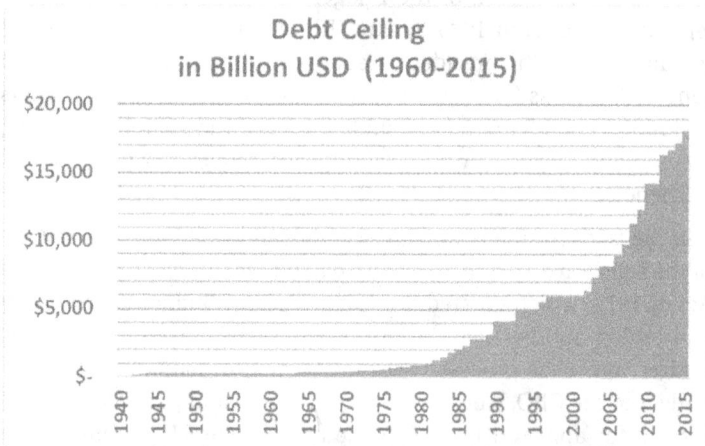

Source_ Data from the CRS Report for Congress, The Debt Limit: History and Recent Increases, D. Andrew Austin, Government and Finance Division.

Figure 49: Debt Ceiling Percent Increase (1960-2015).

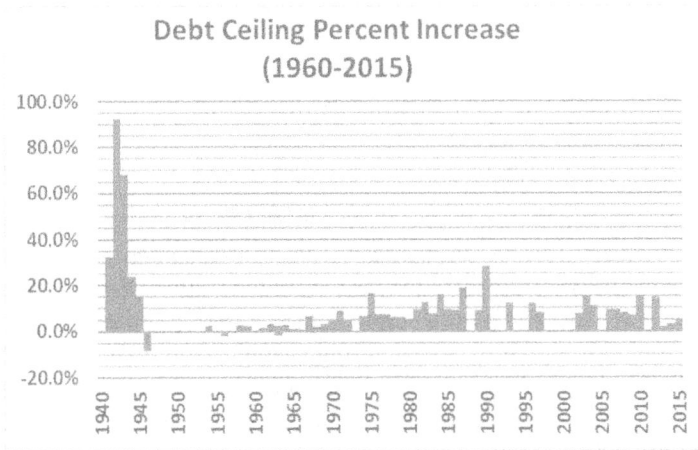

Source: Data from the CRS Report for Congress, The Debt Limit: History and Recent Increases, D. Andrew Austin, Government and Finance Division.

The increases started coming more regularly, sometimes multiple times in a year. This coincided with the previously mentioned rise of national debt after R. Nixon lifted the Gold Standard. *Since 1962, Congress has increased the limit 74 times and briefly suspended it three times.* The latest suspension came the day before the Treasury reached the limit during the fiasco of 2015 and will expire in March of 2017. If history serves right, one thing is certain, after a period of posturing and grandstanding from both sides, come March 2017 the debt ceiling will rise again.

Technically, the debt ceiling does not control or limit the federal government from running deficits or incurring obligations. Rather, it limits the ability to pay obligations already incurred by prohibiting the US Treasury from disbursing funds past the ceiling, except for "extraordinary measures." Supposedly, the limit should bring attention to unbudgeted overspending that results in additional unplanned borrowing. Unfortunately, the spending battle has already been lost by then. It is similar to having a radar detector that alerts the driver when the cop just clocked him or her doing 75 MPH in a 55 MPH zone – by then it is too late.

In retrospect, we need to amend the five-step budget process outlined earlier, since, in reality, we have eight steps, with the last three:

Step 6: When spending reaches the budget plan but remains un-
         der the debt ceiling, Congress continues to spend by issu-
         ing public debt instruments and borrowing from IGH

Step 7: If the overspending reaches the debt ceiling, Congress ar-
         gues for a bit then raises the ceiling and continues to
         spend

Step 8: Rinse and repeat

The debt ceiling has turned into a rolling yield sign, in that not
once has it stopped overspending. Many threats and fiscal cliffs
later, Congress plays the same tune every time – they raise the debt
ceiling (or suspend it for a period until they can negotiate a higher
limit). Not approving a raise to the ceiling would force a federal
default that would most likely send the domestic economy into
short-term disarray. Globally, the value of the dollar and the credit
rating of the US would also suffer. While a stark result, however, the
painful reality of why the debt ceiling never once stopped overspending is rooted in "good ole fashioned" politics. To halt the
overspending would require for Congress to trim the fat out of the
budget in the first place. The current system makes it excessively
convenient to reach into the pockets of the Social Security pot-o-
gold. Moreover, Congress not raising the ceiling implies that the
looming fiscal cuts could directly affect their constituents, which
would then lower their chance of re-election significantly. Everything comes back to the underlying motives.

Chapter 9

Debt interest & impending doom

We briefly touched on the interest portion of the debt earlier. However, to frame the debt interest story entirely, we need to add to the discussion the monetary policy levers that the Federal Reserve Bank (FRB) has used early and often to incentivize the economy. The Federal Open Market Committee (FOMC), which is the Federal Reserve's primary monetary policymaking body, has three primary instruments at their disposal: Open Market Operations, the Reserve Requirements, and the Discount/Federal Funds Rate.

The most often used mechanism in their toolbox, the Open Market Operations, refers to the buying and selling of US government securities by the Fed. By hoarding or loosening securities, the Fed inversely influences the level of reserves in the banking system. Lower reserves in the banking system increase the funds available for lending and investment, thereby expanding the economy. Conversely, higher reserves in the system contract it. Since 2008, the Fed has used a form of open market operations termed quantitative easing (QE). QE becomes a useful tool for the Fed when interest rates approach zero, which has been the case since 2008. By purchasing short-term, long-term, and mortgage-backed securities, the Fed promotes increased lending and liquidity to banks.

The Reserve Requirement, and the least used apparatus, denotes the requisite physical funds that depository institutions hold in reserve against deposits in bank accounts. Since banks loan money to customers and businesses based on their amount of cash on hand, setting this limit by the Fed adds controls to lending, which again heats or cools the economy.

The last tool, the Discount Rate, sets the interest that banks pay on short-term loans from a Federal Reserve Bank. The Discount Rate gave way to the Federal Funds Rate in the early 2000s. While the Discount Rate establishes the rate for banks to borrow money from the Fed, the Federal Funds Rates sets the rate for banks to borrow money from each other. The Federal Open Market Committee (FOMC), sets the desired rate via Open Market Operations.

Banks, subsequently, use the Federal Funds Rate to set the Prime Rate, a term recognized by most consumers. The Federal Funds Rate becomes the basis for interest rates on short-term loan products, adjustable-rate mortgages, auto loans, credit cards, home equity loans, and such. The banks express the terms of these loans as Prime plus a certain percentage, depending on the borrower's credit rating, the length of the loan and other factors. Therefore, while the Fed does not set the prime rate directly, they have a huge influence over it. Typically, during a recession, the Federal Reserve drops the rate to increase spending and incentivize a slow economy. Conversely, during an inflationary period, the Fed raises the rate to cool down an overheated economy.

A brief history of Fed time

From the start of The Great Depression and through WWII, the Discount Rate remained below 2%. After lingering between 2-3% during the Rock-n-Roll 1950s, a growing recession from Lyndon Johnson's Vietnam War and overspending in his "Great Society" quest to end poverty and racial injustice, pushed the Discount Rate into the high single digits by 1968.

Figure 50: Federal Reserve Bank Short-Term Rate in Percent (1930-2015)

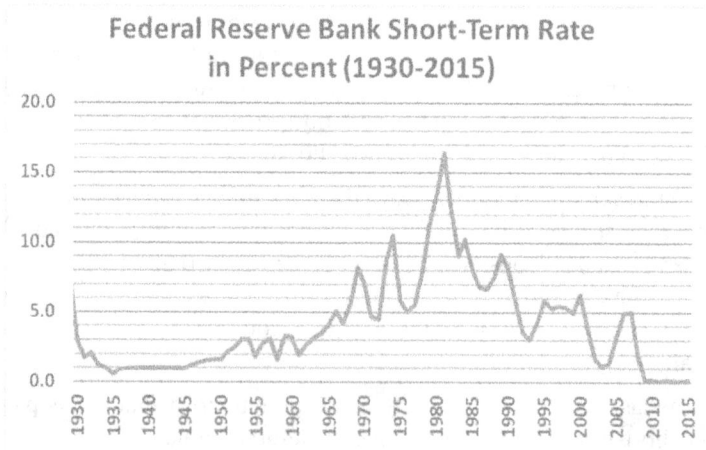

Source: Data from the Federal Reserve Bank, Table H-15 - Federal Funds Effective Rate.

When R. Nixon took office, he pushed out the sitting Fed Chairman, William Martin, who had held the post for 20 years, and nominated Arthur Burns, a supporter of his Keynesian demand-side economic philosophy. In 1971, dealing with a never-ending war, a GDP slowdown, and the tail end of a recession, a desperate R. Nixon and Fed pulled off the triple play which became known as the "Nixon Shock." First, they unlocked the dollar against gold. Second, they placed a 90-day freeze on wages and prices to check inflation. Lastly, they added a 10% tariff on all imports to protect American products against exchange rates. Burns followed by dropping the Discount Rate two full points over a 6-month period. The trick worked like a charm in the short-term, lowering inflation and unemployment, which by the way, came just in time for the 1972 elections. In R. Nixon's words "...he never heard of losing an election because of inflation, but lots were lost because of unemployment."

Figure 51: Short-Term, Inflation & Unemployment Rates in Percent (1950-2015)

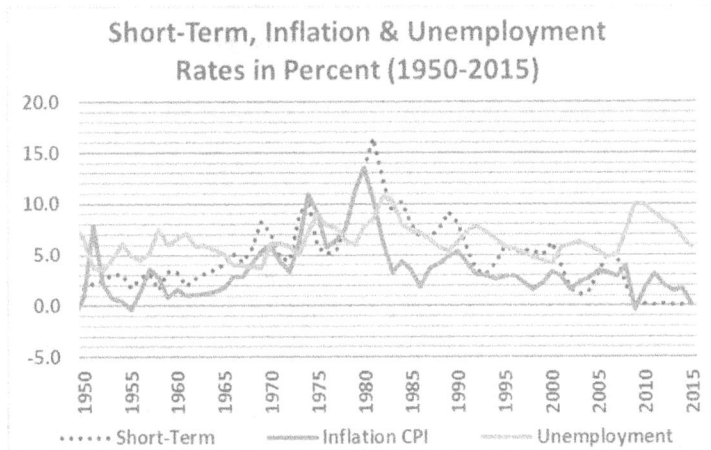

Source: Data from the BLS, Unemployment Rates and CPI Inflation, 1948-2015. Federal Reserve Bank, Table H-15 – Federal Funds Effective Rate.

Well, both inflation and unemployment started to rise after the election and soon we had both in spades, which provided two-thirds of the stagflation recipe. The third and final ingredient came from a sluggish economy due to the 1973 Oil Crisis from the Arab Organization of the Petroleum Exporting Countries' embargo to nations that supplied arms to Israel during the 6-Day War. By 1975, inflation and unemployment had grown to nearly double-digits on their way to even higher levels.

In retrospect, we can see how a multitude of unrelated events aligned like the planets to cause a miserable decade of economic calamity:

- an ongoing Vietnam War
- Tricky Dicky's selfish reasons for an expansionary monetary policy
- a falling dollar from abandoning the Gold Standard
- an OPEC oil embargo in 1973
- the Watergate scandal
- rising inflation and unemployment rates
- another oil crunch in 1979
- and finally, the Iran Hostage crisis

This sequence of events plunged a "not-ready-for-prime-time" VP (shoved into the President's chair when R. Nixon resigned), an overwhelmed southern peanut farmer and a skeptic country knee deep into The Great Inflation of the late 1970s and early 1980s. The runaway economy bottomed out in 1981 with an exorbitant Discount Rate of nearly 20%, to control rising inflation and unemployment rates that peaked at 14.8% and 10.8%, respectively. The unprecedented move to raise the Discount Rate to 20% came from Paul Volcker, the renowned economist appointed Fed Chair by Jimmy Carter in 1979.

In summary, Arthur Burns held the Chair from 1970-78 and stoked the inflation fire. Short lived Chair, William Miller (1978-79), then tossed kerosene on it, setting up the stage for Volcker. Paul, the Godfather of the modern Fed, attacked The Great Inflation with unheard of tactics by raising the Discount Rate to unparalleled levels, then favoring Open Market Operations after he got the economy back on track. His strategy worked.

However, a new sheriff had come into town by 1981, and he had an entirely new set of ideas on how to put America back on top. The former actor, Ronald Reagan, entered the political scene from stage right and his fiscal policies would earn many nicknames over the years: Reaganomics (by broadcaster Paul Harvey), Voodoo Economics (by 1980 Republican candidate and his future VP, George H.W. Bush), trickle-down economics, supply-side economics and even free-trade economics.

R. Reagan's supply-side revolution had started a few years earlier, with a napkin sketch from economist and advisor to President Gerald Ford, Arthur Laffer. His sketch of tax rate versus tax revenue began with the premise that the government received zero tax revenue if the tax rates were 0% or 100%. At 0%, the government did not collect taxes, and at 100%, the incentive to produce disappeared. However, somewhere in between 0 and 100 hides the optimal tax rate that will produce maximum revenue. Before Laffer, the prevailing theory held the belief that higher taxes resulted in greater revenue. To achieve the maximum inflection point on the Laffer curve, the government would have to incentivize businesses and individuals to work hard but not to the point of overtaxing.

Figure 52: The Laffer Curve proposed by economist Arthur Laffer

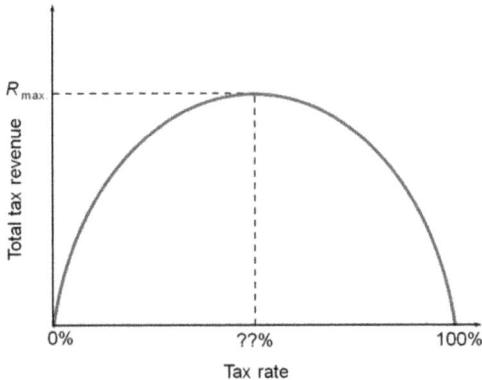

Source: Data from The Laffer Center, The Laffer Curve

Unlike the government aided demand-side Keynesian philosophy, R. Reagan's trickle-down economics focused on incentivizing the high-end of the supply-side by lowering taxes, which in theory would grow the economy and "trickle-down" to the rest of the tiers. His tactic attacked the GDP equation from the consumption angle. By lowering taxes, he would increase consumption which would, in turn, increase investment.

GDP = Consumption (1 – Tax Rate) + Investment + Gov't Spending

R. Reagan also supported government deregulation and Volcker's tightening of the money supply to lower inflation. Even though The Gipper succeeded in pulling the country out of The Great Inflation (with Volcker's help) by putting Americans back to work and facilitating the economic trend that led the country into the prosperous

1990s, he most definitely failed in reducing government spending. In fact, he set new heights for overspending with an average deficit of ~5.0% of the GDP over his tenure. Not since WWII had the country seen such high deficits. However, similar to WWII, but on a much lower scale, raising the government spending increased the GDP (refer to the previous equation), which ultimately helped the economy by adding jobs. Therefore, from a high level, we can make a strong argument that his trickle-down approach worked. During his two terms, he grew the job market by 21 million jobs, the Dow doubled after stagnating for the previous decade, and the GDP grew at an aggressive ~7% clip, all of this while lowering inflation and unemployment.

Figure 53: Spending – Mandatory vs. Discretionary as Percent GDP (1970-2015)

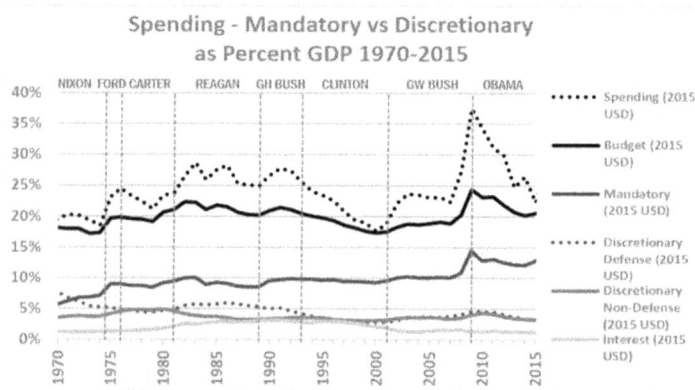

Source: Data from the White House Office of Management and Budget, Table 8.1 – Outlays by Budget Enforcement Act 1962-2021

The previous chart showed the government budget and spending before and after the R. Reagan years, and how the overall federal machinery increased as a percent of the GDP, which stood opposite his "reduced spending" rhetoric. His budgets kept mandatory spending flat, lowered non-defense discretionary spending but increased military spending, thereby pushing the overall budget past 20% of the GDP. However, the *actual* expenditures raced past 25%, reaching levels not seen since FDR.

Figure 54: Effective Tax Rates by Quintile in Percent (1980-2005)

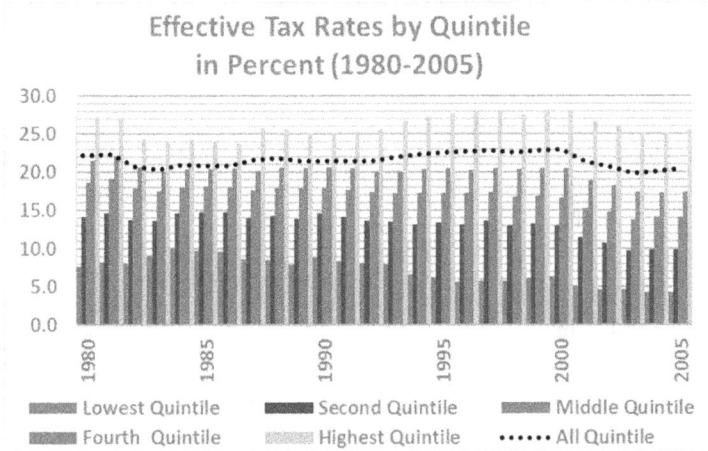

Source: Data from the Congressional Budget Office, Table 1A - Effective Federal Tax Rates for All Households, by Comprehensive Household Income Quintile, 1979-2005

Meanwhile, as far as taxes, R. Reagan initially dropped the overall effective rate from 22% to 20% via the Economic Recovery Tax Act of 1981. His tweak to the tax receipts, the Tax Reform Act of 1986, slowly grew the rates back to the 22% rate by the end of his second term, where they remained through the administrations of G.H.W. Bush and B. Clinton. As advertised, R. Reagan reduced the taxes of the Top-20 percentile (Highest Quintile in the previous chart) while the Middle-60 stayed about the same. The rates of the Bottom-20 increased initially by 27.5% but came back down to the starting level by the time Bush Sr. took over.

In 1987, Ronald Reagan appointed a new Fed Chairman, Alan Greenspan, when the highly-respected Paul Volcker stepped down after two terms. Greenspan paid immediate dividends after he minimized the effect of the Black Monday 1987 market crash, when the Dow and the S&P 500 shed more than 20% in one day. The Fed Chair quickly stepped in to assure the markets firmly stating "...its readiness to serve as a source of liquidity to support the economic and financial system." In only two days, the market recovered about half of the losses from Black Monday, ushering in a new era of investor confidence in the Fed's ability to manage and quickly correct market downturns. This, in turn, would facilitate the economic boom that would transpire over the next decade.

When George H.W. Bush took office, he inherited a rising deficit from R. Reagan that forced his hand to go back on his campaign promise of "Read my lips, I will not raise taxes." He raised taxes on the upper brackets – a very unpopular move that amounted to political suicide. He did the right thing for the country at a very high personal cost that ended up losing him the 1992 elections to a slick sax-playing governor from Arkansas. Bill Clinton maintained most of G.H.W. Bush's tax policy, which he then cashed in during the rise of tech, providing him with unprecedented tax receipts from higher effective rates at the upper end.

By the mid-1990s, Greenspan did not want to screw up a good thing, so he left the Discount Rate untouched at ~5%. After all, as we discussed earlier, the market took off abruptly in the dot-com exuberance. When the economy slowed down after Y2K, and in the aftermath of September 11, Greenspan dropped the rate to ~1%, which unbeknownst to him, in combination with the repeal of the Glass-Steagall Act, turned on the afterburners on "The Big Short" – the coming housing market crash. In 2004, when he finally realized that the light at the end of the tunnel was an oncoming freight train, he tried to correct the course and raised the rate back to 5% over a two-year period. However, by then it was too late, so he did the only reasonable thing he could – he retired, the weasel, and left the next chairman, Ben Bernanke with an absolute mess. When the housing market crashed in 2008, the new Fed Chair quickly dropped the discount rate from 5% to below 0.25%, where it has remained since 2009.

(ASIDE: With the Enron, Tyco and WorldCom scandals from the early 2000's and then the housing crash later in the decade, Congress got busy devising safety measures to undo some of the S&L deregulation from the 1990's. The 2002 Sarbanes-Oxley Act overhauled regulatory standards in response to accounting malpractice. In 2010, the Dodd-Frank Wall Street Reform and Consumer Protection Act closed loopholes, partially reinstated the Glass-Steagall Act as the Volcker Rule (yes, named after the former Fed Chair and a supporter of B. Obama), and established several new government agencies tasked to oversee various aspects of the banking system. The biggest responsibility, however, comprised of monitoring the financial stability of major banking and insurance firms deemed "too big to fail." Behemoths that fell into this category included AIG, the Bank of America, Citigroup, JP Morgan, Wells Fargo, GMAC, Goldman Sachs and Morgan Stanley – each of which received between $10-67 billion as part of the $700 billion bailouts of 2008. By the way, that $700 billion did not include the bailout of Fannie May and Freddie Mac, Government-Sponsored Enterprises (GSEs) in the secondary mortgage market, which accounted for another $187 billion. All this new regulation put in place oodles of additional controls.)

With the Fed Funds Rate hovering at historically low levels since 2009, the Fed ran out of moves on one of their three apparatuses since they literally could not drop the rate any lower. Technically, the Fed could have resorted to negative interest, replicating the temporary strategy used by the European Central Bank (ECB) recently. In this upside-down scheme, borrowers get paid, and savers get penalized – weird, right? Scared European investors, instead of spending, hoarded cash since it would cost them money for the bank to hold it, which slowed the EU economy even more.

The Fed, instead of following the ECB path, chose to implement a quantitative easing strategy to help banks with liquidity, or the ability to convert quickly a valuable into spendable cash. QE has succeeded in proving that no matter how much money the Fed threw into the system, they could not stop deflation, which held ground well below 2%. The economy, on the other hand, grew at a tepid rate since 2010. Unemployment dropped by half (not really but we will discuss this later) since peaking near 10% while the Dow had more than doubled since the bottoming out in 2008. Hence, in 2016, the rate has begun to trickle slowly up the curve along with not so subtle hints and innuendo from the new Fed Chair, Janet Yellen, that higher rates are coming sooner than later. Trump going into office has also stoked the higher rates fire as he has big, huge, great vast plans for the economy.

The cost of borrowing

Not surprisingly, the interest portion of the debt also started to climb in the 1970s when R. Nixon eliminated the Gold Standard. R. Reagan opened the floodgates on overspending in the 1980s, at a time when the country had just come out of The Great Inflation with interest rates that peaked at an exorbitant 20+%.

So, why is this chapter titled "...Impending Doom"? Well, because the chronic government overspending since the 1970s has created an imminent fiscal disaster if the debt continues to grow at the current rate. *The Fed Funds Rate cannot stay below 0.25% forever, so* *imagine what will happen to the interest portion of the debt when the rates start rising again while the debt balance sits at $20+ trillion.*

Figure 55: Debt Interest vs. Short-Term Rate in Billion USD (1962-2015)

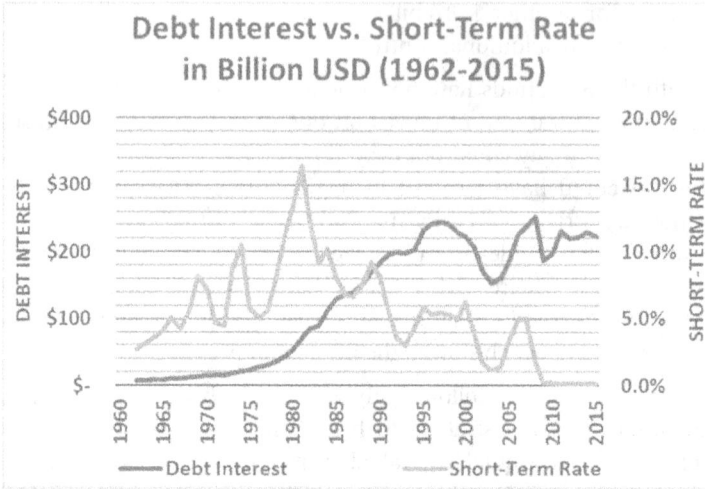

Source: Data from the Federal Reserve Bank, Table H-15 - Federal Funds Effective Rate

Figure 56: Debt Interest Maturity Distribution in Million USD – 2015

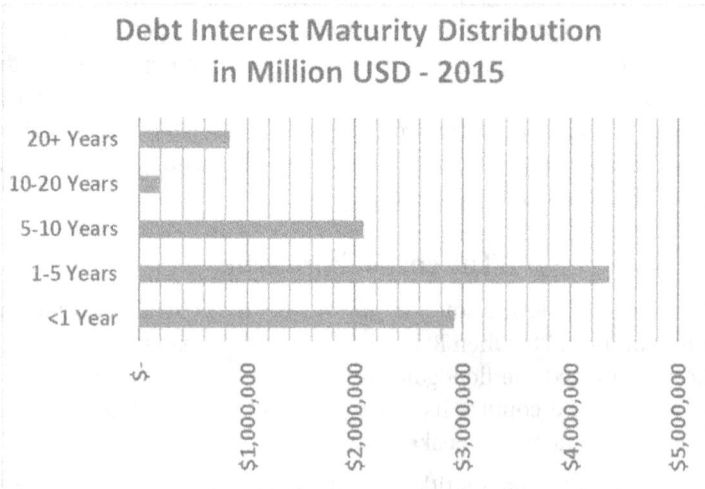

Source: Data from the Fiscal Treasury Bulletin, Table FD-5—Maturity Distribution and Average Length of Marketable Interest-Bearing Public Debt Held by Private Investors

The previous charts show the maturity of outstanding interest-bearing debt vs. the Discount Rate since 1962. In other words, the interest rates that we paid for the borrowed debt. The length of the loans run from 3-month short-term to 10-year long-term, while the average term amounts to 61 months. By fooling ourselves into thinking that we ONLY spend 6% of the GDP on interest, we do not take into account how quickly the interest payments will balloon if inflation were to drive the rates to say 5% or 10% or, perish the thought, 15+% like in the early 1980s. By 2026, the CBO anticipates that long-term 10-yr and short-term 3-month interest rates will increase from 2.2% and 0.1% to 3.6% and 2.9%, respectively. Their analysts also expect the GDP will grow from $17.9 trillion in 2015 to $27.5 trillion by 2026. *At that pace by their calculations, we will reach a $500+ billion interest payment by 2020 and a $1 trillion payment inside of a decade.* There're no two ways about this – that is a horrid scenario. Just imagine what the budget could fund with that kind of cash! We could quadruple the funding for programs for Education, Healthcare, Housing, and Veterans benefits.

This scenario with the ridiculously low Discount Rate seems eerily reminiscent of when the Barleycorns played the "introductory" Annual Percentage Rate (APR) game by rolling over their credit card balances to a new card at an initial rate of 0.9% for 6-months. This sounded great on paper, but on month seven when the APR ramped up to 24.9%, they quickly found themselves in even deeper doo-doo than before. Now their monthly payments rose to even higher levels than their previous cards that had a 19.9% APR, further limiting their ability to pay down the principal balance.

Chapter 10

Analysis by President & Party

Now that we have exhaustively looked at the overall budgets and spending of the US and the history behind it, let's get down to brass tacks and see who should shoulder the blame as the worst offenders in the ever-growing national debt. We will break down the budgets, spending and accumulated debt by presidents and political parties to see which ones can lay claim to economic progress or, alternatively, fiscal doom.

Up until now, we have talked mostly in nominal dollar values, which clearly display the exponential progression of revenue, spending, debt, GDP, etc. Because the amounts have grown considerably since the times of G. Washington, from the millions to the billions and now into the trillions of dollars, in order to compare fairly over time, first we need to adjust the numbers to normalize their worth. We will make three adjustments to the annual values for spend:

1. <u>Percentage of GDP</u>: Accounts for spending relative to the GDP. Since the GDP has a direct correlation to the population of the US, this normalization indirectly performs a "per capita" adjustment.

2. <u>Inflation</u>: Tallies for monetary inflation using the Consumer Products Index (CPI) published by the Bureau of Labor Statistics. We normalized values into equivalent 2015 US dollars.

3. <u>Annual Mean</u>: Addresses the length of presidential tenure so that we can fairly compare FDR (14 years) to Kennedy (3 years) to one-term and two-term presidents.

One quick housekeeping note, in 1976 the government switched the end of the fiscal year from June to September. While the feds still list this "transitional quarter" in all the publications, they do not include the budget accrued during that period to either 1976 or 1977. As with the government and standard economic practice, we will also ignore this quarter from our analysis because it has a negligible impact on the overall statistics.

Budgets & spending

The next two charts capture the federal budget and spending by President normalized by annual amount. The first chart once again illustrates the exponential growth and progression of the GDP and budgets/spend over time. We can also observe the gap between the GDP and the budget/spend curves narrowing since FDR. Similar to the Barleycorn household, the expenses have continued to climb as Jonathan and Maria have received salary increases over the years. They bought a house, two new cars, Frankie started college and let's not forget the annual week-long "family vacation" over the summer to Disney World. Just like with the federal government, the costs add up quickly, raising the bar on expenses over the years.

Figure 57: Annual Federal Budget & Spending by President in Billion 2015 USD

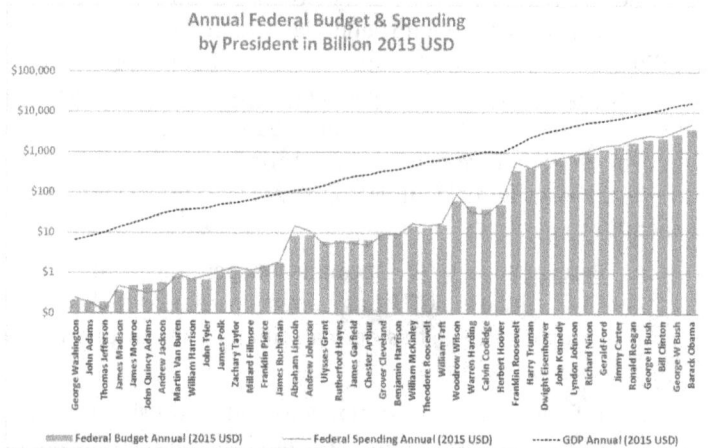

Annual Federal Budget & Spending
by President in Billion 2015 USD

Source: Data from the White House Office of Management and Budget, Table 1.2 – Summary of Receipts, Outlays, and Surpluses or Deficits as Percentages of GDP. Conversion to 2015 USD using CPI from US Dept. of Labor and Statistics.

Figure 58: Annual Federal Budget & Spending by President as Percent GDP

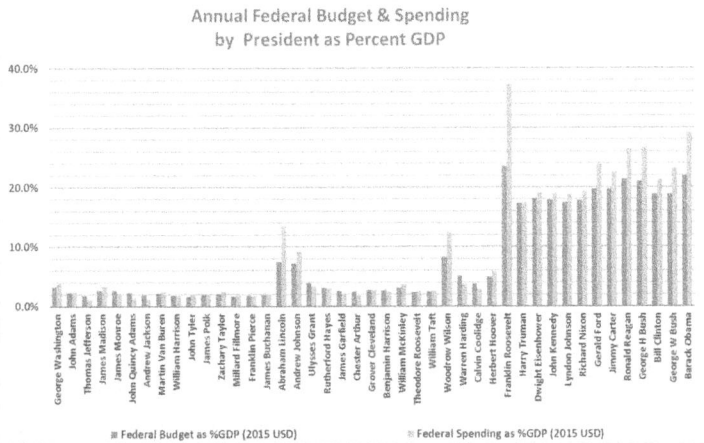

Annual Federal Budget & Spending
by President as Percent GDP

Source: Data from the White House Office of Management and Budget, Table 1.2 – Summary of Receipts, Outlays, and Surpluses or Deficits as Percentages of GDP. Conversion to 2015 USD using CPI from US Department of Labor and Statistics

The second chart shows the budget and spending as a percent of the GDP. We can draw three conclusions from this graph:

1. We have had three distinct periods in American history with respect to government budgets and spending to GDP (budget percent, spending percent):

   a. Independence to Civil War (2.1%, 2.1%)

   b. Civil War to Great Depression (4.1%, 4.8%)

   c. Great Depression to present (19.5%, 23.4%)

2. Three wars stuck out like seismic events in the cost timeline – the Civil War, WWI, and WWII

3. FDR raised the roof on government spending with his New Deal programs

Figure 59: Federal Budget and Spending as Percent GDP

President	Political Party	Federal Budget as % GDP	Federal Spending as % GDP	Comment
Franklin Roosevelt	Democratic	23.5%	37.3%	The Great Depression & World War II
Barack Obama	Democratic	21.9%	29.2%	Afghan War, Iraq War II, The Great Recession
Ronald Reagan	Republican	21.3%	26.4%	
George HW Bush	Republican	20.9%	26.7%	Iraq War I
Gerald Ford	Republican	19.7%	23.8%	
Jimmy Carter	Democratic	19.7%	22.6%	The Great Inflation
George W Bush	Republican	18.8%	23.1%	Afghanistan War & Iraq War II
Bill Clinton	Democratic	18.8%	21.3%	
Dwight Eisenhower	Republican	18.1%	19.0%	Korean War
John Kennedy	Democratic	17.9%	19.0%	
Richard Nixon	Republican	17.8%	19.3%	Vietnam War
Lyndon Johnson	Democratic	17.4%	18.8%	Vietnam War
Harry Truman	Democratic	17.3%	17.3%	World War II

Source: Data from the White House Office of Management and Budget,
Table 1.2 – Summary of Receipts, Outlays, and Surpluses or Deficits as
Percentages of GDP. Conversion to 2015 USD using CPI from US Dept. of
Labor and Statistics

Combing for the biggest spenders, as expected from the previous
chart, every president since FDR shows up at the top of the spend
list. FDR sticks out like a sore thumb at the top of the list, but the
Second World War severely skewed his numbers. When we ignore
the years 1942-45 from his time in office, his numbers come in way
higher than his predecessor H. Hoover and below Harry S Truman,
at 10% budget and 15% spend. After the War, the budgets followed
FDR's spending levels going forward in the high teens, then steadily
grew to the current level at ~20%.

After FDR, we can cluster the remaining twelve presidents into
three statistically similar groups:

Group 1: B. Obama, R. Reagan, and G.H.W. Bush

All three budgeted in the 21-22% range while spending 27-29% of
the GDP. B. Obama gets mostly a pass since he inherited a big
housing mess from his Democrat predecessor B. Clinton and one
unnecessary war from W. However, let's not forget that he also
added Obamacare. R. Reagan also inherited an economic mess
from the three stooges (R. Nixon, G. Ford, and J. Carter) but he also
burned a ton of cash strengthening our military. Bush Sr., for the
most part, extended R. Reagan's fiscal policies, then turned around
and raised taxes to lower the debt. His goodwill to do the right
thing for the country did not earn him any favors but did set the
stage for the next dude stepping into the White House.

Group 2: G. Ford, J. Carter, G.W. Bush and B. Clinton

These four budgeted between 19-20% and spent 21-24%. It was unexpected to find G.W. in this grouping – we would have anticipated for him to land in Group 1 since he presided over the expense of two wars.

Group 3: H.S Truman, D. Eisenhower, J.F. Kennedy, L. Johnson, and R. Nixon

It should be no surprise that the pre-1971 Gold Standard Commanders in Chief clustered close together at 17-18% in budgets and 18-19% in spending.

Analyzing the budget and spending data by political party, we evaluated all the presidents by each of the three periods and as a group, going back to their party origins – Andrew Jackson on the Dem side and Lincoln on the GOP side. Relative to the GDP, we compared the overall budgets and spending as well as the portions of debt owed to either public or IGH debt, using a statistical tool called an ANOVA. Shockingly, we find no statistical difference between Democrats and Republicans for any of them – budget, spending, public debt, or IGH. The analyses had p-Values greater than 0.5 across the board, which translates into strong conclusions. Overwhelmingly, *when it comes to budgets, spending, public debt, and IGH debt as a percent of the GDP, it does not matter which party occupies the White House.*

This conclusion defies logic based the enormous size of the debt accrued by B. Obama. The debt grew more under Barack's watch than all the presidents before him combined. However, we need to calibrate his huge debt numbers back to the size of the economy while also considering inflation. From a percentage viewpoint and relative to the GDP, B. Obama ran similar debts to those of R. Reagan and G.W.H. Bush, which counterbalanced the overall analysis.

In summary, since WWII, the budget has run at ~20% of the GDP – that seems to be the burn rate for the post-FDR welfare entitlement society. The spending, however, has grown at an alarming rate since we abandoned the Gold Standard and did not put controls in place to limit the overspending. Since 1975, G. Ford's last two years of R. Nixon's second term, the spending has averaged ~25% of the GDP. *According to the data, the economy of the US has demanded a ~25% budget since G. Ford, yet every year the White House has spun ~20% budgets which then forced an average ~5% deficit since 1975.*

The ugly truth is that the tax revenue bucket needs to increase to match the actual spending of the country in the last 40 years. The other option, reducing the budget to 20%, carries way too much political inertia to get anywhere in Washington.

OK, so that covers the overall budget and spending, but what about how presidents spend their budgets? Surely Republicans spend more in military and Democrats on welfare, right? Well... perhaps, and we will cover that next.

Category analysis by President

In this chapter, we will break down the spending outlays of presidents and political parties for the ten categories established by the Budget Enforcement Act.

The next chart shows the progression of budget spending by category and by the presidents since 1933. The bars in each cluster align chronologically from left to right by the president, starting with F. Roosevelt and ending with B. Obama. Each cluster of bars represent the top 7 categories, which accounted for more than 99% of the total spend: Defense, Pensions, Health Care, Interest, Welfare, Education and Transportation.

Figure 60: Federal Budget by Category by President as Percent GDP (1933-2016)

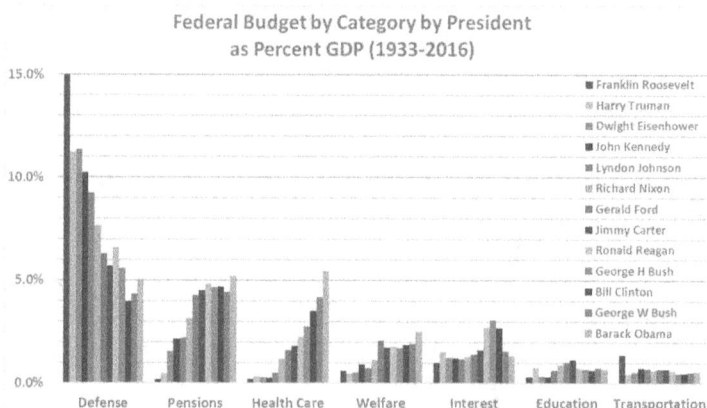

Source: Data from the White House Office of Management and Budget, Table 1.2 – Summary of Receipts, Outlays, and Surpluses or Deficits as Percentages of GDP. Conversion to 2015 USD using CPI from US Department of Labor and Statistics.

The last three categories, General Government, Protection, and Other each accounted for less than 0.5% of the GDP, so we ignored them in the by-president analysis. The General Government category included federal courts and administrative services and took $43.7 billion (0.25% of GDP) per year to operate in 2015. The Protection bucket accounted for federal aid to police, fire responders, and prisons but accounted for only $30 billion (0.17% of GDP). The Other group comprises a host of departments such as forestry, hunting, fishing and waste management, the largest of which received less than half of the funding of General Government.

Defense

In the chart above, we clipped the first bar of the Defense category slightly to enhance the rest of the graph (F.D. Roosevelt's defense bar grew to 17% of the GDP due to WWII). The clear trend from the Defense bar cluster lies in the enormous reduction in military spending since FDR, which bottomed out during B. Clinton's administration at ~4% but ratcheted back up since to ~5% of the GDP. Considering the state of the War on Terror, this bucket does not appear that it will come down below ~5% anytime soon. By the way, the fifth bar from the right that breaks rank from the descending progression belongs to Ronald Reagan. However, for all of his reputation as a tough, commie-hating, non-compromising military spending machine, he only spent ~1% more of the GDP than his predecessor.

Pensions

This cluster consists mostly of Social Security and, to a lesser extent, the pensions for Federal and Military employees. This chart partially tells the story of why Social Security is in deep trouble. The bars grew at a rapid pace from F.D. Roosevelt to G. Ford; then the growth has flattened out since then. We will double-click on Social Security in the Loose Ends chapter.

Health Care

So here's a news flash. Every president since Ike has spent more on Health Care than his predecessor, regardless of party affiliation. Obamacare pushed Barack's bar slightly higher, but like R. Reagan on the military, he spent only ~1% of the GDP over the prevailing trend, and nowhere nearly as high as the rhetoric from Tanner and his merry band of ACA haters. The trend in this category, however, looks to remain for the near future as Trump will have to deal with the rising costs of premiums. The ACA consists of two components – the privately paid health insurance premiums and the Medicare supplements to people who cannot afford them. This latter component cost taxpayers $35 billion in 2015, $46 billion in 2016. The OMB projects the cost of the ACA to mushroom to an average of $90+ billion for each the next four years. All of which, according to Skye, is money well spent on needy Americans.

Interest

Interest ranks as the fourth largest category by spend. Now, we covered the debt interest payments in detail in the previous section, but this chart adds more weight to the "impending doom" hypothesis. The interest payments peaked during periods of high interest rates during the R. Reagan, G.H.W. Bush, and B. Clinton administrations. Even though by B. Clinton's second term the Discount Rate had dropped to ~5%, the interest payments lag about five years due to the maturity of the debt instruments. In the last 16 years, the interest has hovered well below 5%, and for the last eight years at a ridiculously low <0.25%.

Welfare

Similar to Health Care, the Welfare bucket has grown steadily for the last 80 years. Two presidents stick out a little more than the rest, LBJ and B. Obama. Johnson pushed his bar higher than the trend, with his social spending and (unsuccessful) quest to end poverty. B. Obama's welfare bar also pushed higher, but some of his expenses came from the boatload of money that he was forced to spent on market-crash recovery, particularly on unemployment benefits and food stamps. After his first term, the B. Obama welfare numbers fall in line with the expected trend growth.

Education

What sticks out the most in this category is how little we spend on Education – an average of 0.7% of the GDP. From D. Eisenhower to J. Carter the bars trended slightly upwards, peaking at 1.2%. However, since then, the spending has dropped by nearly half and remained at that 0.7% level since R. Reagan took office, which somewhat explains why the US currently ranks 17th in the world in Education. If we only had more money to spend on Education. Oh, wait, we do – did we mention how much cash we burn every year on debt interest? Ugh.

Transportation

How little we spend on transportation ranks as another area of concern for the US. The big bar on the left, at 1.4%, belongs to FDR as he, in an effort to put Americans back to work, instituted numerous New Deal programs to build public works, i.e., roads, bridges, airports, and dams. Since then, the budget has hovered at 0.6% of the GDP. Given the growth of the population and the current state of our aging infrastructure, most experts agree that the Transportation category is in dire need of additional funds (Bechtel, 2015). Fortunately, D. Trump has promised to spend $1 trillion over the next four years rebuilding our infrastructure, which would more than triple the current budget.

Education and Transportation rank as the forgotten categories. Like the saying goes: *If we had some ham, we could have ham and eggs. If we only had some eggs.*

Category analysis by Party

Looking at the same categorical data by party (in the chart below) shows very similar results to the last section where we discussed differences (or lack thereof) between the overall budgets by the presidents. Basically, there does not seem to exist a huge difference between parties in how they spend the budgets.

Figure 61: Federal Budget by Category by President as Percent GDP (1933-2016)

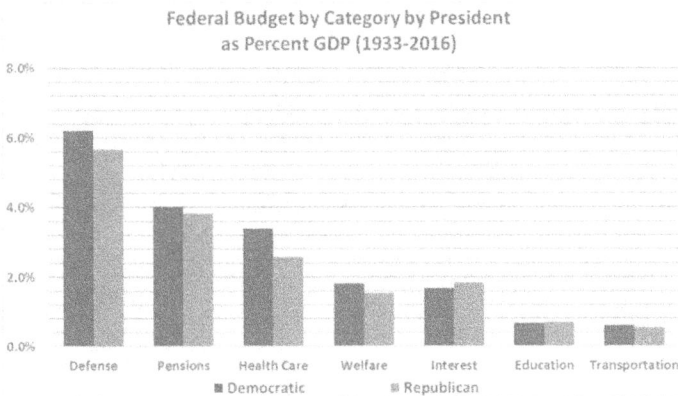

Federal Budget by Category by President as Percent GDP (1933-2016)

Source: Data from the White House Office of Management and Budget, Table 1.2 – Summary of Receipts, Outlays, and Surpluses or Deficits as Percentages of GDP. Conversion to 2015 USD using CPI from US Dept. of Labor and Statistics

Boosted by the gargantuan military spend during WWII, the Democrats spent more than Republicans on Defense. If we remove FDR from the analysis, the bars even out on military spending. Likewise, the values for Pensions, Interest, Education and Transportation rank as statistically the same, or not different in statistical parlance.

Health Care stands as the one area where it appears that the Democrats have significantly outspent the Republicans. However, when we consider the linear growth of the spending (each president since Ike spent more than his predecessor), the party of the latest president will always skew this chart to their side. If we re-evaluated the performance by a political party after G.W., the Republican bar would rise higher. We can make the same argument for Welfare – remove B. Obama's contributions, and the Republican bar grows taller than the Dems.

So, we are back to the same conclusion as before. *It does not matter who presides or which party is in office with respect to how we spend the budget.* Overwhelmingly, large-scale episodes, such as wars and seismic economic events, have dictated how administrations spent the budget.

Chapter 11

Loose ends

In this chapter, we will delve into a few related economic topics that typically get lots of press coverage such as wealth distribution, unemployment as well as some key programs that suck up a lot of funds and resources such as Social Security, and the Department of Homeland Security.

Wealth distribution

Let's start by discussing the gap between the "haves" and the "have-nots." We will present the wealth and income distributions of the US population, which per the data has widened significantly over the years.

Figure 62: Share of the Wealth by Percentile (1989-2013)

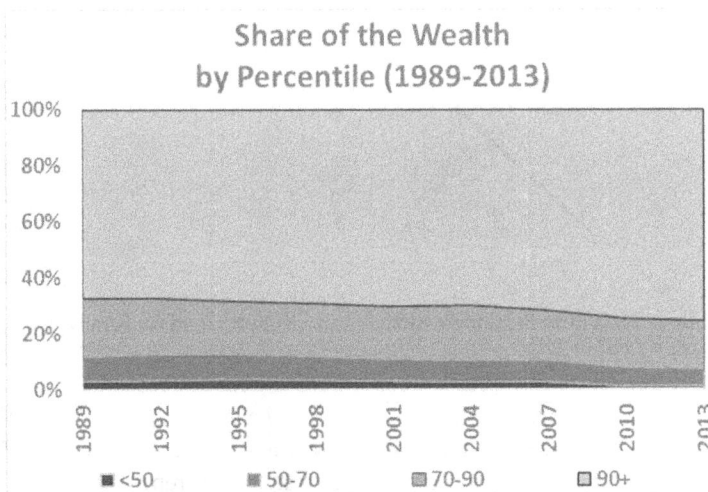

Source: Data from the Congressional Budget Office, Trends in Family Wealth, 1989 to 2013

The previous chart, published by the CBO, shows the distribution of family wealth by four percentile groups: <50, 50-70, 70-90 and >90 percentiles. The CBO has published this study every three years since 1989 and defined wealth as assets minus debt. Assets include home equity, investments, bank balances, pension accounts and business equity. Debt comprises credit cards, car loans, and student loans but excludes mortgages.

By their analysis, the top 10 percentiles of the US population held 75.0% of the wealth in 2013, an increase of 7.5% when compared to the 67.5% they held in 1989, and which came at the expense of the other groups. The 70-90 percentiles group lost ground, from 21.4% to 17.7%, as did the 50-70, from 8.2% to 5.6%. The bottom 50 percentiles of the US owned less than 1.1% of the wealth in 2013, down from 2.9% in 1989. The CBO expects the gap between the top and bottom to widen when they publish the 2016 study.

Figure 63: Lorenz Curve of Wealth Inequality (1989-2013)

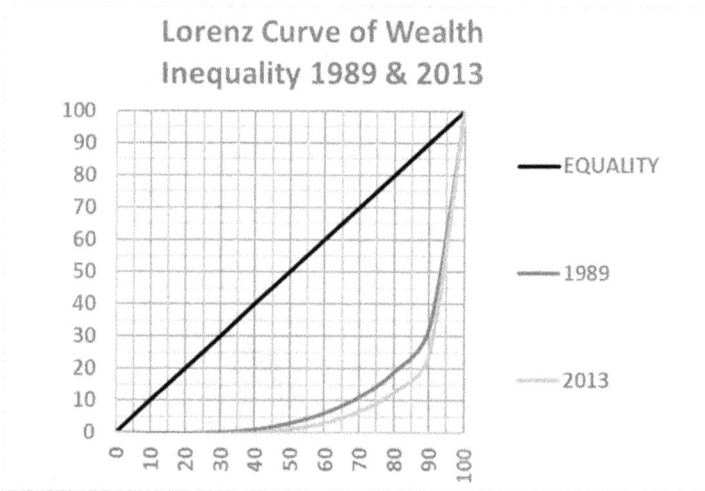

Source: Data from the Congressional Budget Office, Trends in Family Wealth, 1989 to 2013

The Lorenz curve in the previous chart, developed by Max Lorenz, graphically depicts the distribution of wealth by the percentile of the population (Kleiber, 2007). The straight line represents a perfect Marxian equality, where every percentile holds an equal amount of the wealth. The actual distribution of wealth in the US keeps growing wider with the area above the Lorenz curve and the below the Equality curve increasing from 1989 to 2013.

Income distribution

When we analyze the wealth gap by income, the outcome looks pretty much the same as the wealth distribution. In a study published by the US Census Bureau, comparing the median income after taxes for the five quintile groups from 2000 to 2011, the rich get richer while the poor get poorer. The median income of the top two groups, at the 70th and 90th percentile, increased their wealth by about 10%. Meanwhile, the middle 50th percentile bucket spent their time treading water losing only ~7%, the 30th percentile lost ~50%, and the lowest 10th percentile bracket got walloped, losing more than 500%.

Figure 64: Median Income by Quintile (2000-2011)

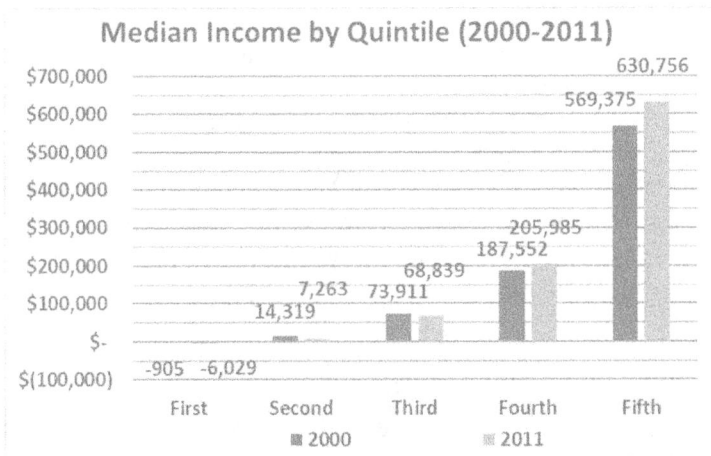

Source: Data from the U.S. Census Bureau, Survey of Income and Program Participation, 1996 and 2008 Panels

There is no question that the gap has widened between the "haves" and "have-nots." From accumulated wealth to income distribution, everything points to the wealthiest, and specifically the top 10% of Americans, owning a disproportionate amount of the wealth in the US.

Gini Coefficient

Since statisticians frown upon small sample sizes, both previous analyses depended upon limited points in time and did not necessarily explain what happened in between. We do not want to fall into the "rising gun death in Australia" statistical trap described in the Preface. So, we need a better way to depict the change in time, which we found in an obscure metric from an Italian economist named Corrado Gini.

One simple manner to express the inequality of wealth distribution uses the Gini Coefficient derived from the Lorenz curve (Lamb, 2012). The Coefficient establishes a number between 0 and 1 as the ratio of the area above and below the Lorenz curve and represents a measurement of the statistical dispersion of wealth between the upper and lower classes. This metric also works for income or assets distribution.

The Bureau of Labor Statistics (BLS) has published the annual value for the Gini Coefficient since 1947. The trend in the following chart shows the widening gap growing at a quadratic pace since bottoming out in the 1960s. As we can see from the correlation curve below, the ratio between the haves and have-nots bottomed out around 1970, and the classes have continued to grow apart ever since. While Democrats like to point the finger at R. Reagan and his trickle-down economics as the beginning of the separation between the classes, the trend started at the inflection point when the US decoupled from the Gold Standard, which also marked the time that we started to accumulate debt at an increased rate.

Figure 65: US Gini Coefficient (1947-2015)

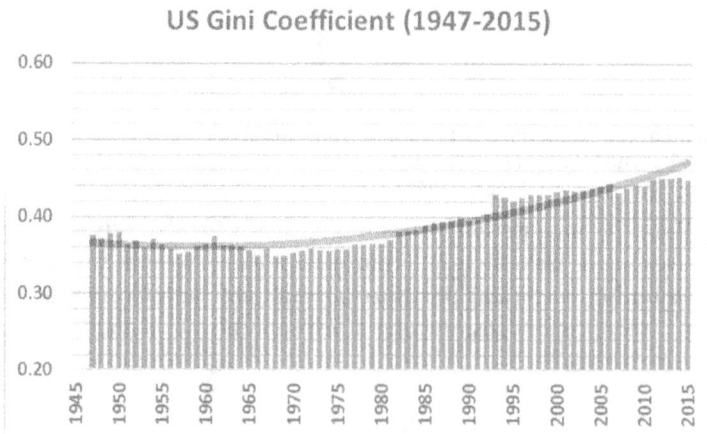

US Gini Coefficient (1947-2015)

Source: Data from the Bureau of Labor Statistics, Table F-4. Gini Indexes for Families, 1947 to 2015

Unemployment

The current monthly-published unemployment rate report system began in earnest in 1940, as part of the decennial census, by the New Deal's Works Progress Administration. The WPA turned it over to the Census Bureau in 1943 and then to the BLS for good in 1959. The implementation of a formal unemployment metric came from FDR's need to understand the progress of the jobless situation during The Great Depression. Since 1915, the BLS had been estimating the unemployment rate with very limited and rudimentary statistical processes. The 25% jobless claim at the height of The Great Depression came closer to an educated guess and may have peaked even higher.

The monthly survey that started in 1940, called the Current Population Survey (CPS), established the basis for the official detailed statistics for unemployment (Bregger, 1984). Initially deployed to 8,000 households, the CPS currently employs a statistically comprehensive and robust survey of 60,000 households across the US to estimate the size of the employed and unemployed worker pool.

Let's begin by defining some terms that shape the unemployment story and have had a significant impact on its outcome. The work pool comprises the superset of the 16-and-over US population that could potentially hold a job. The labor force, also called the civilian labor force, consists of the employed and the unemployed. The employed includes workers that received pay for part-time or full-time work, as well as those that worked 15 hours or more, paid or unpaid, for business or farm, run by a family member with whom they live. The unemployed comprise those that currently have no job but actively looked for one in the last month. Persons that have no jobs and are not looking for jobs do not count towards the labor force. Typical folks in this camp would include the 16-and-under demographic, college students, retirees, stay-at-home folks with family responsibilities, persons unable to work due to a disability as well as the unattached workers (formed by the marginally attached and discouraged workers).

The term marginally attached refers to former laborers that are not currently employed but want to work and have looked for a job in the last 12 months. Discouraged workers include persons that have stopped looking for a job because of lack of job availability in their field, lack of training for the jobs available, or discrimination, such as too old.

The BLS also modifies the unemployment rate by a seasonal adjustment factor, meaning that they erase the fluctuations of seasonal events such as changes in weather, harvests, major holidays, and school schedules.

Unemployment metrics

The next chart depicts the "official rate" since 1948, but there is a lot more to this story since the way we measure this metric has changed several times to improve its accuracy.

Figure 66: US Unemployment Rate (1948-2016)

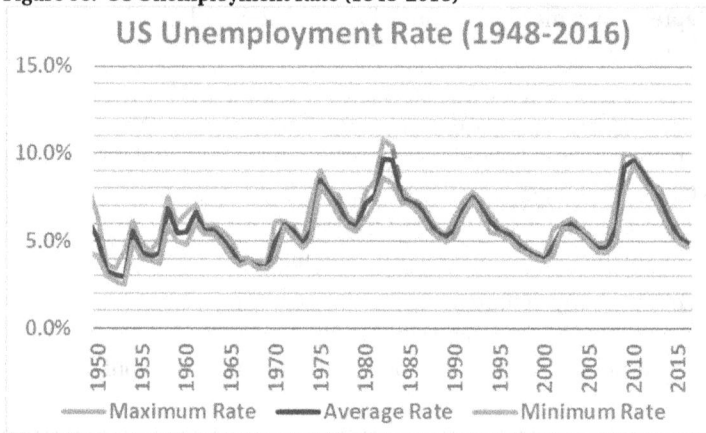

Source: Data from the Bureau of Labor and Statistics, Unemployment Rates, 1948-2015

Since it started tracking unemployment, the BLS has continued to tweak and improve the methodology for the calculation of the rate. Continued questions about how to more accurately measure marginally attached workers eventually led to the implementation of multiple classifications to further define the unemployed. In the 1970s, the BLS introduced a new U1 to U7 classification, which became the precursor to the current U1 to U6 system implemented in 1994 and still in use today (Bregger, 1995):

U-1: Persons unemployed 15 weeks or longer

U-2: Job losers and persons who completed temp jobs

U-3: Total unemployed (*official unemployment rate*)

U-4: U3 plus discouraged workers

U-5: U4 plus those marginally attached to the labor force

U-6: U5 plus part-time workers for economic reasons

Figure 67: Unemployment Rate, U1-U6 (1994-2015)

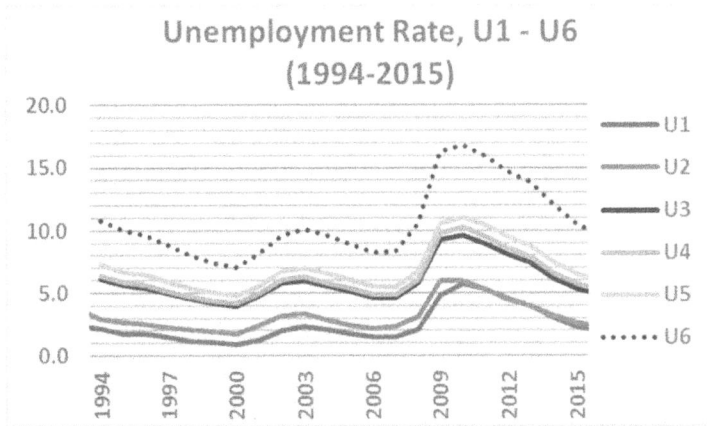

Source: Data from the Bureau of Labor and Statistics, U1-U6 Unemployment Rates, 1994-2015

The current official unemployment rate, U3, does not include the marginally attached and discouraged workers in the metric. The U6 includes those two groups as well as those working part-time for economic reasons and depicts a vastly more complete canvas of the unemployment picture. However, given the option, any politician would choose to report the lower of the two numbers to make their metrics look better, which explains why the government has always reported the U3. At the end of 2016, the U3 stood at 4.6% versus the U6 at 9.4%.

The next chart shows the rates of the individual unattached workers by categories: discouraged workers, marginally attached and part-time workers. The first group, the number of discouraged workers that have stopped looking for work, doubled in 2010 and remained at ~100k. The second group, the marginally attached workers still searching for jobs in the last 12 months, has remained relatively flat at ~100k. The third group, part-time workers due to economic reasons, shows a huge increase in those wanting full-time work but forced to take part-time gigs. The level sat at ~400k from 1994 to 2007, peaked at 878k in 2009 and dropped to 631k in 2015. The preliminary numbers in 2016 maintain it at ~600k.

Figure 68: Unattached Workers by Type (1994-2015)

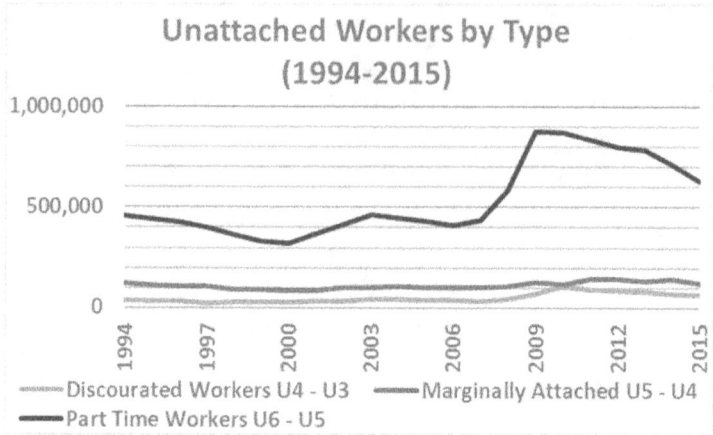

Source: Data from the Bureau of Labor and Statistics, U1-U6 Unemployment Rates, 1994-2015

But here's the rub – part-time workers count as employed in the U3 metric. Also, there is one uncounted group in all these metrics – persons that took a lesser paying job out of necessity.

Measurement modifications

Over the years, the BLS has changed the unemployment metrics upon the recommendation of the Division of Employment and Unemployment Analysis. Every mathematician knows that there are two ways to lower a ratio – either decrease the numerator (the unemployed workers) or increase the denominator (the job market). So, what did they do? In 1983, they changed the measurement of the metric by adding the Armed Forces stationed stateside to the equation, which added 1.7 million workers to the job market (increased the denominator) and lowered the rate by 0.2% points. Even though this study began in 1979 under J. Carter's administration, R. Reagan became the beneficiary of the nominal change in the rate.

A similar event occurred in 1994. This time, under new president Bill Clinton, the BLS revamped the metrics to the current U1 to U6 format. The long and the short of it is that, without changing anything, the bean counters redefined how to classify the beans once again. Here's what they did: they kept the U1 and U2 as is, eliminated the old U3 and U4, renamed the old U5 to U3, the old U6 to U4, the old U7 to U5 and created a new U6 metric based on the old U7.

The new U6 redefined the marginally attached worker's bucket by limiting the time looking for a job to one year. This modification reduced by ~700,000 the number of marginally attached workers (decreased the numerator) which lowered the new U6 over the old U7 by ~0.5%.

It is almost like we need a decoder ring to keep up, but to summarize, the old U5 became the new U3 and the old U7 morphed into the new U6, which looked better on paper by ~0.5%. If you are confused, don't worry – you are not alone. When nothing else works, change the measuring stick.

Jobs created

In addition to the jobless rate, the BLS maintains a massive database of economic data, which includes a view of total jobs annually going back to 1939. We can use this database to analyze the number of jobs added annually and evaluate performance by presidents and by party.

Figure 69: Total Jobs Non-Farm in Thousands (1940-2015)

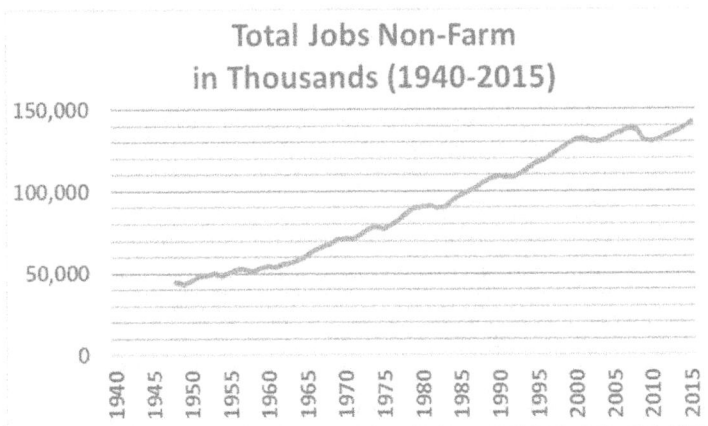

Source: Data from the Bureau of Labor and Statistics, Jobs Created, 1939-2015

Using the measure of jobs created as a percent of the job market (in the next chart), Jimmy Carter would rank as a great president, when he presided over one of the worst economic stretches since The Great Depression (a mess passed to him from R. Nixon, by the way). FDR and H.S Truman benefited from the skyrocketing WWII job machine that boosted their job creation numbers to the top two spots on this list. R. Reagan's job numbers looked healthy and would have rated even higher had he not inherited two years of negative growth, as the result of The Great Inflation. Bill Clinton, on the other hand, benefited from the tech boom, which boosted his job number to the 4th highest since H. Truman. In summary, job creation is a poor indicator of economic progress by the president, so we need a better metric.

Figure 70: Percent Jobs Created by President (1940-2016)

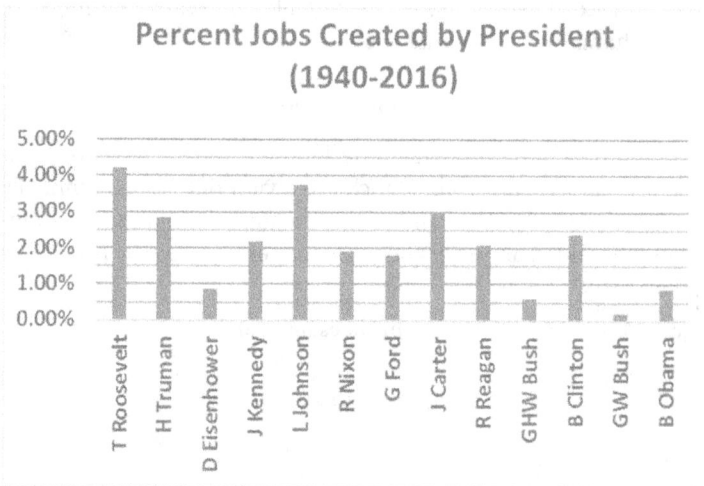

Percent Jobs Created by President (1940-2016)

Source: Data from the Bureau of Labor and Statistics, Total Nonfarm Jobs Created, 1939-2016.

Since the job market has increased over time in a manner proportional to the growth of the population, we cannot use the total jobs added at their face value. We need to normalize the data. But how? We could use the percent of jobs added in relation to the job market, but would not fully capture the growth of the workforce population. Ultimately, we care about the number of jobs available relative to those that could work, i.e., the work pool made up of the 16 and older demographic.

Figure 71: Jobs Created by Number and Percent (1948-2016)

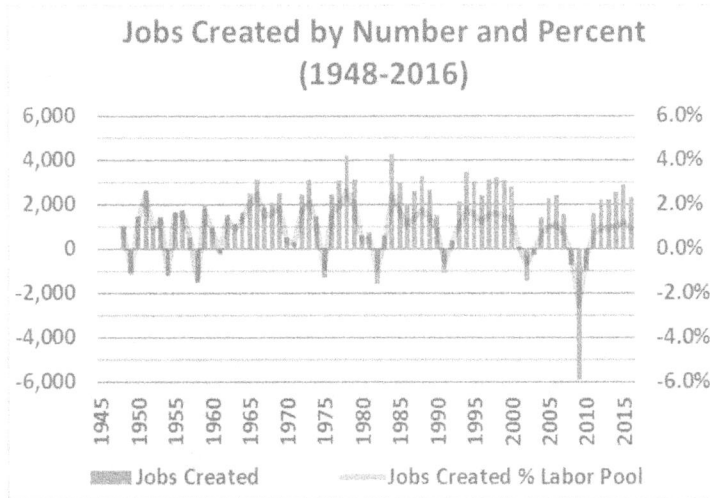

Jobs Created by Number and Percent (1948-2016)

Source: Data from the Bureau of Labor and Statistics, Jobs Created, 1948-2015

The previous chart, depicting the annual jobs created by total number and percent relative to the labor pool since 1948, shows why this metric does not do justice to the effectiveness of a particular presidency. Up and down years of the US economy, in the form of inflationary and recessionary periods, have a large impact on the job market. Moreover, as we have discussed ad infinitum, most of the time, the acts that lead to these types of events usually take place years before, sometimes decades. Take the examples of G.W. Bush and B. Obama. G.W. Bush inherited the dot-com and 9/11 recession, then the housing crash and ensuing Great Recession, which also affected B. Obama. These two events, unrelated to their administrations, severely skewed their job numbers. Outside of those two events, their administrations generated jobs at about the same rate, ~1%.

The stark reality

So, why does it feel like even though the unemployment rate sits at a low of 4.6% at the end of 2016, that the job situation is not that great? The answer to this question is complex but lies with the unattached workers, the shrinking labor force, the aging American population and the type of jobs available.

Figure 72: U6 minus U3, Unattached Workers (1994-2015)

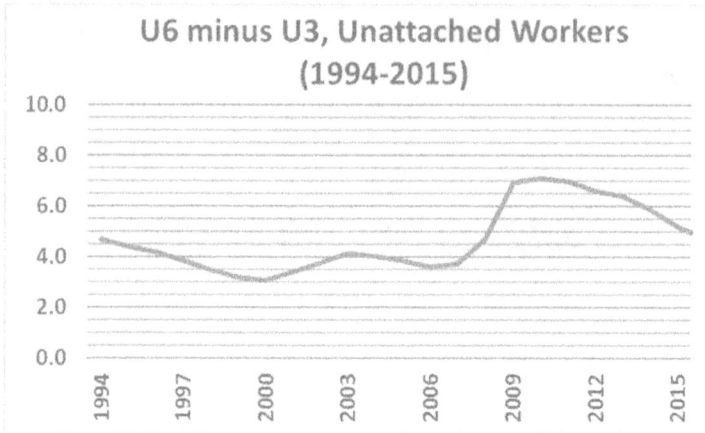

Source: Data from the Bureau of Labor and Statistics, U1-U6 Unemployment Rates, 1994-2015

The first factor, the unattached workers, we can identify readily by the difference between the U3 and U6 rates. The previous chart shows how the chunk of unattached workers, including discouraged and part-time workers, increased significantly in 2008, peaking in 2010. Since that time, it looks like the rate of unattached workers has dropped almost back to the ~4% level from 2007, but we need to dig further because there is more to that metric.

The second factor involves the shrinking labor force. The U3 jobless rate has dropped consistently, from a high of ~10% in 2010 during the peak of the Great Recession, dipping below 5% in 2016. However, the ratio of the labor force to the 16 and over age group, which forms the basis for the labor pool, has shrunk by ~ 4%. In other words, the labor pool has continued to grow at a steady rate, in line with the rise in the US population. The labor force, on the other hand, has flattened significantly.

In the below chart, we can ascertain how the ratio of the labor force to the labor pool grew from ~60% in 1948 to a peak of ~67% during the tech boom of the 1990s. After the dot-com and 9/11 recession, the ratio dropped one point to ~66% until 2008 when it started to drop precipitously to the current level of ~63% in 2016. *This decrease of ~3% since 2008 translates to roughly 8.1 million former workers that have become "The Forgotten" in the unemployment statistics.*

Figure 73: Labor Force vs. 16+ Population Labor Pool in Thousands (1948-2015)

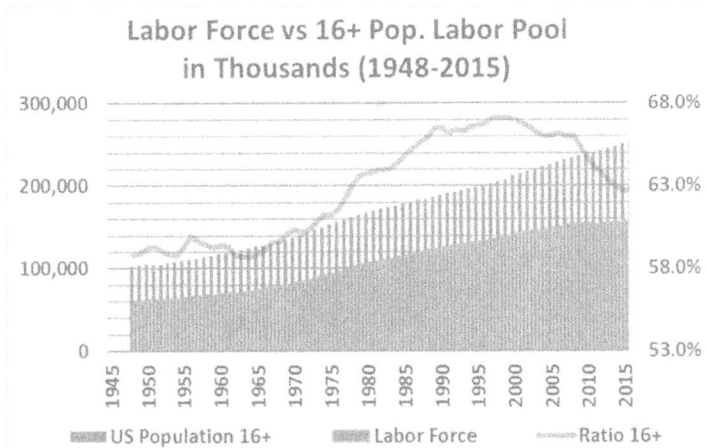

Labor Force vs 16+ Pop. Labor Pool in Thousands (1948-2015)

US Population 16+   Labor Force   Ratio 16+

Source: Data from the Bureau of Labor and Statistics, Household Data Annual Averages, Employment status of the civilian non-institutional population, 1945 to date

According to the Pew Research Center, nearly 20% of Americans are working past the retirement age in 2016, about twice the level from 1990 (Desilver, 2016). Several reasons exist for this trend, but longer life expectancy in combination with financial necessity rank as the leading causes. With work benefits shrinking and pensions all but evaporated, retirees that failed to build up a significant retirement nest egg cannot make ends meet on Social Security alone, which forces them to continue to grind.

Since the timing of the decrease of the job pool coincided with the Baby Boomers starting to reach retirement age (66 years old in 2012), let's see what the force-to-pool ratio looks like if we eliminate the 65+ population from the work pool.

The next chart, depicting the force-to-pool ratio versus the 16-to-64 demographic, shows a similar trend. In 1948, the ratio stood at ~64% and grew steadily until reaching a peak of ~77% in 1988; then it stayed flat until 2008. Since 2008, similarly to the previous analysis, the ratio has retreated ~4% to ~73%. We can conclude from these numbers that the retiring baby boomers do not explain away the missing labor force from the work pool.

Figure 74: Labor Force vs. 16-64 Population Labor Pool in Thousands (1948-2015)

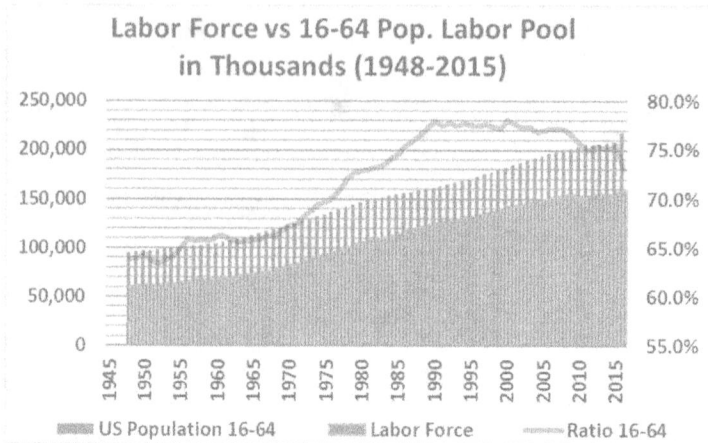

Labor Force vs 16-64 Pop. Labor Pool in Thousands (1948-2015)

US Population 16-64   Labor Force   Ratio 16-64

Sources: Data from the Bureau of Labor and Statistics, Population of 16+ Age Group and Civilian Labor Force Levels, 1948-2015.

Then, why is the labor force shrinking? This downtrend goes back to the definition of the unemployed and the marginally attached. The U3 metric only counts unemployed persons that have actively searched for work in the last month and does not include marginally attached workers. The U6 does count the marginally attached but only those persons looking for a job in the previous 12 months. "The Forgotten" fall into that category. Baby Boomers forced to take early retirement against their wishes or younger persons that cannot find work in their fields and prefer to pass on either part-time work or lesser paying jobs.

Other factors contributing to the reduction in labor force include extended unemployment insurance, extended SNAP benefits and ACA employer coverage. Most states will pay for unemployment insurance for up to 26 weeks. In 2008, Congress enacted legislation to extend federal dollars to help those most affected by the recession. Two programs extended the unemployment insurance benefits: the Emergency Unemployment Compensation (EUC) and the Extended Benefits (EB). The EUC had four tiers that offered 6-20 weeks of additional benefits to workers that had exhausted their state's benefits. The EB added another 13 weeks on top of the EUC. Congress extended both programs as part of the American Taxpayer Relief Act of 2012, and they finally expired in 2014. Through similar legislature, the SNAP program also extended additional benefits to the unemployed.

The last factor considers employers that maintained part-time workers to avoid paying health insurance. Per the ACA website, "if the employee works less than 30 hours a week, or less than 130 hours in a month, they are considered part-time under the law (for the purposes of being offered coverage by their employers). While somewhat speculative in nature, the timeline for the ACA kicking into gear, October 2010, overlaps the rise of part-time employees, which peaked in 2009 but remains as the bulk of the U6 "part-time for economic reasons" jobless classification.

Social Security

Let's get something out of the way – Social Security (SS) is not broke. In fact, SS will never go broke as long as the federal government continues to take payroll taxes from the paychecks of American workers. The Social Security Trust Fund (SSTF) is another story entirely. The SSTF accounts for the accumulation of payments by Americans into SS over the years. In other words, up until now, people paid more into the SS fund than those that collected benefits. That, however, will come to an end in the near future as the rising number of Baby Boomers reaching retirement age will outnumber the folks contributing to the fund. If we never repay the $2.8 trillion we have borrowed from the SSTF, we will consume the current fund balance of $2.9 trillion in the next 20 years or sooner, if we continue raping, err, borrowing from it annually.

SS benefits

How are SS benefits calculated? The amount received depends on how much and how long the recipient has contributed to SS. A recipient receives the maximum amount when he or she has contributed for 35 years and then waited until the full retirement age of 66, which used to be 65 and will soon change to 67. One can start to receive benefits at age 62 at a reduced portion of the full amount. The Social Security Administration (SSA) prorates the benefits from 75% to 100% for retirement between ages 62 and 66, progressively.

The SSA calculates the amount of the benefit based on the inflation-adjusted average earnings for the highest 35 years contributed to SS. If a person did not contribute to SS for 35 years, then the calculation assumes $0 earnings for those years. Accordingly, the payment can increase if a recipient delays the payment up until 70 years old.

So, if a person emigrated to the US and started to contribute to SS at age 48 when he or she retired at age 66, he or she would only receive about half of the maximum benefits. It is a very fair system based on individual contribution, so disregard all the bogus rumors from Tanner claiming that illegals receive SS checks. Never have. Never will.

SS Fund history

As we mentioned earlier, the SSTF consists of the Old-Age and Survivors Insurance (OASI) and the Disability Insurance (DI) funds. FDR established the OASI Trust Fund in 1937, as part of the Social Security Act, while the DI Trust Fund came into existence in 1957.

The next charts show how the annual receipts (money collected from payroll taxes) will catch up to the expenditures (benefits paid to beneficiaries) on the OASI fund in the next couple of years, whereas DI already crossed that line in 2008. In the OASI chart, we can identify when we began to borrow funds in the mid-1980s by the flattening portions of the "Total Receipts" curve. Had the pre-1985 slope of the curve continued, the "Total Expenditures" curve would not catch up to the "Total Receipts," and we would probably not be discussing this topic right now.

Figure 75: OASI Trust Fund Receipts and Expenditures in Thousands (1937-2015)

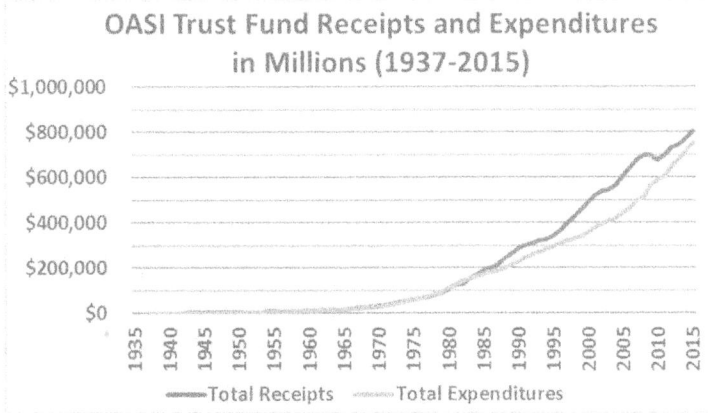

OASI Trust Fund Receipts and Expenditures in Millions (1937-2015)

Source: Data from the Social Security Administration, OASI Trust Fund 1937-2015, DI Trust Fund 1957-2015

Figure 76: DI Trust Fund Receipts and Expenditures in Millions (1957-2015)

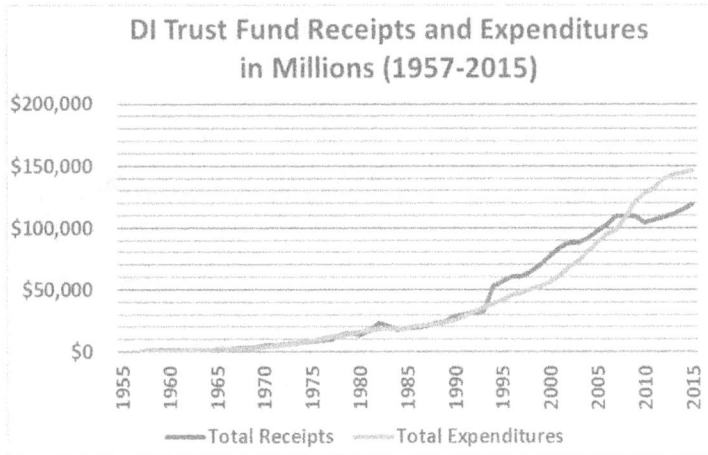

DI Trust Fund Receipts and Expenditures in Millions (1957-2015)

Source: Data from the Social Security Administration, OASI Trust Fund 1937-2015, DI Trust Fund 1957-2015.

When we look at the cumulative Asset Reserves of the funds in the next charts, we can readily assess how we will exhaust the DI trust fund by 2017 and how the OASI will peak the in the next couple of years and then follow the same trend as the DI. The SSA estimates that we will empty the OASI Trust Fund by the mid-2030's.

Figure 77: OASI Trust Fund Asset Reserves in Millions (1937-2015)

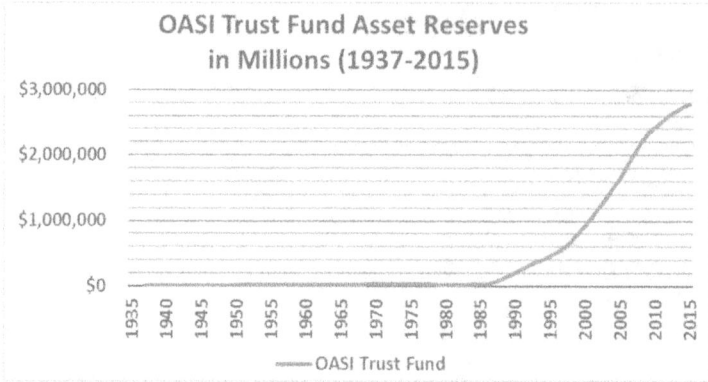

Source: Data from the Social Security Administration, OASI Trust Fund 1937-2015, DI Trust Fund 1957-2015

Figure 78: DI Trust Fund Asset Reserves in Millions (1957-2015)

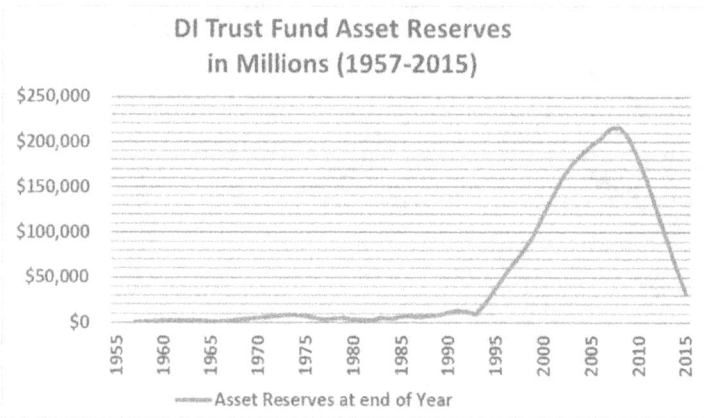

Source: Data from the Social Security Administration, OASI Trust Fund 1937-2015, DI Trust Fund 1957-2015

The following chart tells the Baby Boomer story, those born between 1946 and 1964 when the US population spiked after WWII. In the Beneficiaries chart, the change in slope in the curve that occurs in 2008 points to the first wave of Baby Boomer babies born in 1946 that took early retirement at age 62.

Figure 79: Beneficiaries Receiving Social Security Benefits (1970-2015)

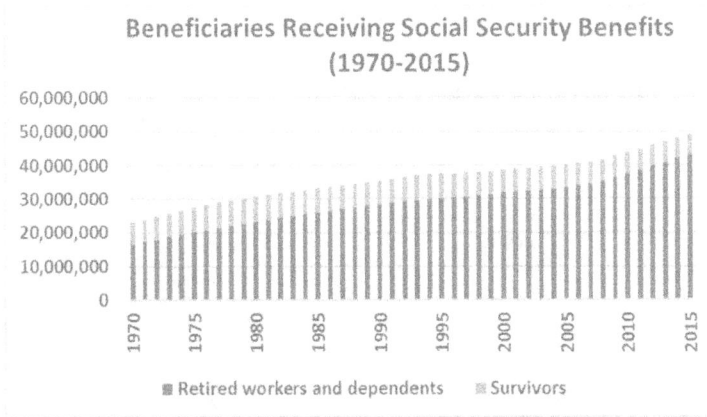

Beneficiaries Receiving Social Security Benefits
(1970-2015)

■ Retired workers and dependents ■ Survivors

Source: Data from the Social Security Administration, Number of beneficiaries receiving benefits, 1970-2015

Figure 80: US Population Annual Growth (1900-2010).

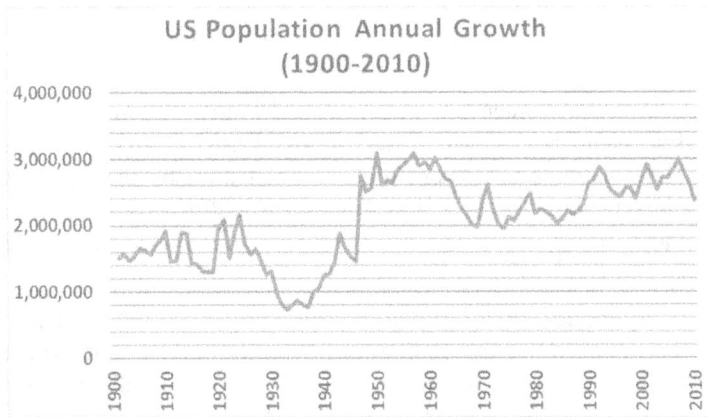

US Population Annual Growth
(1900-2010)

Source: Data from the US Census, Population Growth 1900-2010

The second chart, showing the annual growth of the US population since 1900, shows the Baby Boomer population spike who recently became SS recipients. In the mid-1960s, the population stabilized and had grown steadily since at a ~1% rate. In 2015, about 50 million Americans claimed SS benefits.

One more significant factor has exacerbated the SS equation – life expectancy. Per the Census Bureau, in 1930 when FDR established the Social Security Act, the average American male lived to the ripe old age of 58.1 while his female counterpart lived to 61.6. Since that time, advances in medicine have extended the life expectancy by nearly two decades.

Figure 81: US Life Expectancy (1930-2010)

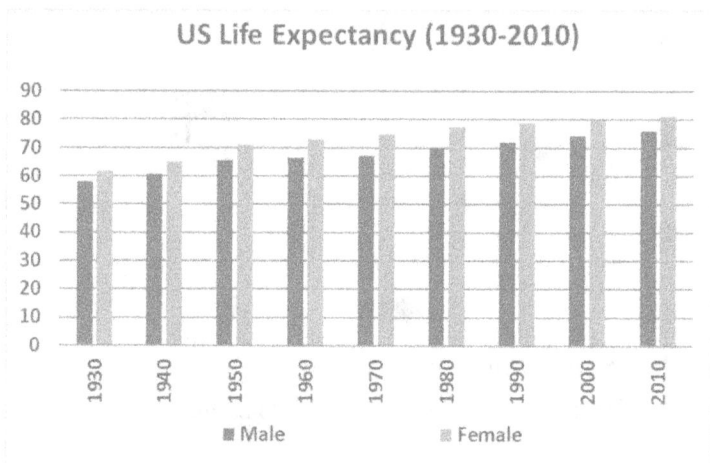

Source: Data from the US Census, Population Growth 1900-2010

By 2010, the average American man and woman lived to 76.2 and 81.1 years old, respectively. This continued rise has added tremendous strain on a SS system that assumed that the beneficiaries would start to collect at 65 years old but would not live much past that age. Today, on average, a 66 year -old retired beneficiary would collect for about 12 years.

To accommodate for the increased lifespan of recipients, R. Reagan pushed for the 1983 Social Security Amendment, which changed the retirement age from 65 to 67 implemented over a 22-year period, and increased the payroll tax contribution. Those born after 1960 will have to wait until age 67 for full benefits. However, the 1983 Amendment came at a time when the life expectancy had increased by ten years as compared to 1930. Since then it has grown by another eight years, which explains the ongoing discussions of increasing the retirement age again, this time to 72 years old.

So what does this all mean?

It says that the combination of the Baby Boomer population spike becoming SS age eligible, longer life spans and the continued borrowing from the SSTF has created a situation that will drain the fund by the mid-2030s. Once we deplete the SSTF, we can only count on the annual collection of payroll taxes to fund the benefits due, which will force a reduction of benefits to the recipients. Current estimates from the SSA project that starting in 2034, the benefits may shrink by as much as 25% to beneficiaries. This spells doom for the vast majority of recipients that do not have other nest eggs or pensions and depend solely on Social Security for retirement. For most of them, this translates into continued employment well into their seventies to make ends meet. *Alternatively, we repay the money we borrowed from the SSTF with interest, and this problem goes away for a long, long time.*

Homeland security

Since the department's creation in 2001, as of 2015 the US had spent $548 billion in the Department of Homeland Security (DHS). In 2016, the gross annual budget of the DHS ran at a modest $41.2 billion. The scope of DHS, however, has grown considerably and, over the years, consolidated a host of former Defense departments and operations including:

- Office of the Inspector General (OIG)

- U.S. Customs & Border Protection (CBP)

- U.S. Immigration & Customs Enforcement (ICE)

- Transportation Security Administration (TSA)

- U.S. Coast Guard (USCG)

- U.S. Secret Service (USSS)

- Federal Emergency Management Agency (FEMA)

- U.S. Citizenship & Immigration Services (USCIS)

- Federal Law Enforcement Training Center (FLETC)

- Domestic Nuclear Detection Office (DNDO)

While we would all benefit from a Sensitivity Training program for TSA employees at airport security scans, Homeland Security is not an area that can afford cuts. The safety record since 9/11 in stopping large-scale events has been impressive, and we like it that way. However, while only three separate smaller-scale attacks occurred over the first 12 years since DHS was founded, three terrorist events have taken place in the last four years resulting in over 100 deaths:

1. Anthrax Attacks, 2001 – 5 Deaths

2. Beltway Sniper Attacks, 2002 – 17 Deaths

3. Fort Hood Mass Shooting, 2009 – 13 Deaths

4. Boston Marathon Bombing, 2013 – 3 Deaths

5. San Bernardino Attack, 2015 – 14 Deaths

6. Orlando Nightclub Shooting, 2016 – 49 Deaths

Considering that the total 2016 DHS dollars accounted for only 1.3% of the $3.7 trillion federal budget, perhaps we need to reevaluate the investment in this department. Bearing in mind the increased and unending targeting of terrorist organizations around the globe, unlike the annual curtailing of wasteful budgetary spending, the DHS stands in a long line of critical federal departments in need of additional budget.

Chapter 12

Final words

We have covered considerable ground on the state of affairs in Washington and the factors that have affected budgets and spending. We started as an aspiring nation 240 years ago, with mostly a state-driven economy and budgetary process. Our founding fathers insisted on allowing the states to make their own decisions. Over the first 80 years, the nation expanded quickly, and the country found itself divided. The Civil War raised the stakes on the Union, and the post-conflict government doubled in scope and size as the country rebuilt. The nation continued to grow as did the need for more federal involvement to establish the necessary economic infrastructure, which steadily increased the budgets and spending. The final tipping point came after the Roaring 1920s exposed all the weaknesses of a nation in dire need of governmental intercession in the form of social reform and financial oversight. A man destined for greatness emerged to redefine our country's future from the polio-driven discomfort of a wheelchair. Against overwhelming financial odds from The Great Depression, and then literally fighting for the future of the world during WWII, the US emerged victoriously, and along the way, FDR established the federal system as we know it today.

In the final analysis, no matter what person or which party presided over our nation, it seems that events of greater importance have molded the spending patterns of the federal government. Wars, as we noted, have had an enormous influence on our nation's debt and deficits, continually ratcheting the bar on spending. The War for Independence brought a hefty price in debt, which took nearly 60 years to pay off. A determined Andrew Jackson took it upon himself to eliminate the national debt, only to see his efforts go to waste in short order. The Civil War, World War I, and then World War II raised the stakes on the debt into the hundreds of billions of dollars. The Korean War, Cold War, Vietnam War, the First Iraq War and then, more recently, the Afghanistan War, the Second Iraq War, and the ongoing War on Terror have driven the national debt to the brink of the $20 trillion mark.

Similarly, large-scale economic events have also had an impact on federal budgets and spending, both positive and adverse. Post-war periods typically brought phases of extended economic prosperity, as the country focused on rebuilding, most notably the Roaring 1920's and the Baby Boomer era after WWII. In the second half of the 1990s, unprecedented tax revenue from the dot-com bubble and tech boom almost generated the first surplus since 1969. On the downside, The Great Depression, The Great Inflation, and the Great Recession have gone down in history as significant markers that shaped the fiscal policies of our nation in the 1930s, 1970s, and 2000s.

Since its founding in 1913, the Federal Reserve, we found, has had a profound and lasting influence in shaping the national economic destiny, also for both good and bad. The initial (and dreadful) response to the market crash of 1929, exacerbated the conditions that extended what could have stopped at a deep recession into a decade-long Great Depression. In the 1970s, the abandonment of the Gold Standard, a counter expansionary monetary policy, a never-ending war and global oil shortages, set off a series of events that led to stagflation then The Great Inflation, peaking with double digit unemployment and interest rates hovering near 20%. Finally, deregulation in the 1990s directly caused the housing bubble a decade later, imploding the market and pushing the economy into the Great Recession.

Our analysis showed that ultimately one factor drives the size of the economy – the exponential growth of the population of the US. More people translates into more consumption, investment, and spending into the economy, which means more production. Regardless of the economic ups and downs over the last 240 years, our nation's economy always bounced back to what seems like a predetermined exponential trend. Therefore, in order to fairly analyze and compare different administrations, we employed the often-used financial methodology of baselining the annual budgets and spending relative to the GDP, while also normalizing for monetary inflation. This technique leveled the playing field so that we could equitably assess and contrast economies across changing times and life during different epochs.

Using this method, we found three distinct eras in the historical budgetary process of the US going back to Revolutionary War. In the pre-Civil War era, the federal budget floated at ~2% of the GDP. From the Civil War until The Great Depression, the government spending increased to ~4%. Then FDR raised the stakes five-fold to the current level of the modern economy, ~20%.

Try as we may lend credence to the political machinery of Republicans and Democrats claiming fiscal and social supremacy, in the end, our investigation proved conclusively otherwise. The budgets, spending and debt compiled by both parties have not differed in the least, going all the way back to their founding presidents, A Lincoln and A. Jackson. It seems no matter which party controls the White House, the budgets and overall spending follow a pre-ordained path.

Not only the overall spending but, surprisingly, also how the GOP and Dems spent money did not differ statistically. Sure, a few presidents temporarily altered the status quo in discrete areas, such as FDR's New Deal, Johnson's War on Poverty, R. Reagan's Star Wars military spending, or B. Obama's Affordable Care Act. However, in the overall scheme of budgets in the trillions, a few billions here or there hardly even registered a significant blip in the overall statistics of the spending timeline.

When we broke down the ten federal budgetary categories by administrations since FDR, we stumbled upon several startling facts. Defense spending has dropped significantly since it peaked at 17% of the GDP during the Second World War, reaching steady state at ~5% since the turn of the 21st century. Pensions, Health Care and Welfare, have continued to grow steadily since FDR and currently account for about 70% of the mandatory spending. Considering the size of the national debt, not surprisingly, Interest now ranks as the fourth highest of the ten buckets. Education and Transportation each earned a pitiful ~1% of the GDP in annual budgets. It is no wonder that our schools and country's infrastructure are in dire need of an overhaul.

We also found how foreign entities own about a third of our debt, with China and Japan owning the largest chunks. The Federal Reserve, in turn, owns 13.6% of the debt, mostly from quantitative easing actions since the 2008 market crash. However, the ever-growing pink elephant in the room continues to raise concerns – we owe IGH ~30% of the debt as of 2015. This never-ending thirst to borrow from Social Security and other government programs looms like a giant ominous cloud.

Finally, we learned that because of the exponential progression of the economy, the most recent president, regardless of party affiliation, will inherit the honor of having spent more money that any Commander in Chief before him. Monetarily, each successive budget ranks bigger than the last. Also, since the debt has grown at a ~5% clip since the 1970s, each president inherited and generated more debt than his predecessor.

So, when it comes to budgets, spending, and debt, disregard the Washington and media pundits expounding on the sins of the administration in power. For the most part, previous events outside the realm of the control of the current tenant at 1600 Pennsylvania Avenue, have molded the fiscal spend years, sometimes even decades, in advance. As much as Tanner and Skye would lead us to believe when it comes to budgets and spending, it hardly matters which party is in charge.

The Barleycorns

Meanwhile, our typical American family, the Barleycorns, find themselves at a crossroads. From the outside looking in, it appears that they have everything – a lovely house, two cars in the garage, the oldest kid in college and a smart and musically creative daughter in high school. They even have the obligatory pet – an ultra-friendly black Labrador named Gavin.

The truth, however, does not come close to resembling a Rockwell painting of old school Americana. In reality, they are up to their eyeballs in debt with no end in sight. If they continue their current path of overspending, they will not only exhaust their retirement nest egg but also end up in bankruptcy court, probably losing their home and valued possessions along the way.

While their current financial dire straits slowly emerged over time, not all their fiscal decisions have been calamitous. Some of the expenses originated from helping their kids plan for a better future – to afford them the education they needed and deserved. Frank, for example, currently attends a state university, even though a more prestigious private school accepted him. After doing some financial acrobatics, they reluctantly decided on the state school, where even with a partial scholarship and student loans, the tuition plus room and board drains them monthly. Not only are Jonathan and Maria strained, but in four years, Frankie will start his working career about $37k in the hole. Welcome to the American Dream.

Roxy, still in high school, has expressed an interest in the performing arts. Her high school music teacher encouraged her to take private piano lessons to improve her chances of getting into Julliard next fall. Maria could not deny Roxy her dreams and pays for the best piano teacher in town with any overtime work she can muster.

Yes, their revenue stream has increased over the years as Jonathan and Maria have progressed in their careers, but ultimately so have their expenses. Their outlays consistently have outpaced their earnings. Also, Jonathan's extended unemployment stint a few years ago, put them behind the 8-ball and, ever since then, it seems, that they have struggled to get back to level ground.

However, they also need to own up to some very un-savvy monetary decisions made over the years, which added drastically to their current situation. Perhaps buying two new cars last year was not in their best interest. They could have driven their older model Chevy and Toyota a little longer. Perhaps they should have re-thought buying that $10k matching living room and dining room set three years ago. They will continue to pay for them for the next two years at a highly unfavorable interest rate because they could not qualify for a better deal due to their poor credit score. Finally, that "investment" in a timeshare several years ago, proved a truly unfortunate decision. The condo maintenance fees have increased to the point that they could stay at a 4 or 5-star hotel for a week for the price they pay for their timeshare's annual maintenance.

So, what can the Barleycorns do to get out from under what feels like an insurmountable mound of financial insecurity? Well, the decision is simple, really. They must spend less and earn more – Budgeting 101. Jonathan and Maria must make some very hard decisions.

Faced with an impending financial disaster and imminent bankruptcy, Jonathan and Maria had a heart-to-heart recently. After thoroughly reviewing their family budget and spending patterns, they decided together that they would stop their monthly over-spending immediately. The scrubbed their monthly expenses and found several areas to save money. They were spending way too much eating out – Maria agreed to make dinner at home during the week while Jonathan would grill on the weekends. Those multiple daily Starbucks runs needed to come to an immediate halt. They would make a pot o' Joe at home in the morning and even started to pack a lunch to work.

They decided that their cars were not worth their $500/month payments, so they would trade-in their cars and temporarily drive older models that would lower their combined car payments from $1,000 to $600/month. They made a decision to sell their timeshare, and even though they would lose their initial invest- ment, it would stop the bleeding of the $1,200 annual maintenance fees.

They scoured every line item in their expenses to prioritize the needs from the wants, the necessary from the unnecessary, the mandatory from the discretionary. Every dollar counted. They prioritized the mandatory spend, i.e., payments required to meet their basic needs of food, clothing, shelter and safety. This category included the groceries, mortgage payment, car payments, home and auto insurance, taxes and such. Even here, they found that they could save money by making prudent choices on the food they ate, the cars they drove and the clothes they wore. Just because it was a necessary expense did not give them a license to overspend in that area.

Then came the discretionary expenses. They struggled at first to agree on what to spend on this category. How much should Jona- than spend attending sporting events or playing golf on the week- ends with his crew? How much should Maria devote to her private Pilates classes, her weekly girls night out, or shopping sprees for her endless shoe collection? After much discussion, they both agreed to curtail their "justified" social outings and discretionary spending by half. It was important for them to maintain some of their social engagements, but not at the expense of their future.

On the other side of the ledger, Jonathan picked up a second job on Saturdays, a temporary part-time gig at a bowling alley, that would add about $400 a month to their revenue stream. They would take every penny of his part-time paycheck to help pay for Frank's college.

They then assembled a 5-year plan to pay down the credit card balances and, more importantly, repay the money they had bor- rowed from their 401k. They figured out that once they put a hard- capped monthly budget in place, that they would use the two extra annual paychecks, from getting paid every two weeks instead of twice monthly, to pay down credit card balances, prioritizing the high-interest cards first. _Going forward, their credit cards would be used as a convenience for paying, not to finance what they could not afford._ They agreed that once they balanced their checking book for a couple of months without overspending that they would treat themselves to dining out once a month (but to an affordable restaurant, nothing fancy).

Eventually, the change in Jonathan and Maria trickled down to their kids. Watching the changes in their parents, Frank and Roxy also decided to get into the act, landing part-time jobs that, even though did not represent much money to the bottom line, would make them productive and contributing members of their household. The monetary tightening of the Barleycorns, in turn, prepared their kids fiscally so that they would not repeat the mistakes of their parents.

While the Barleycorns face some difficult times ahead, if they stick to their plan, they will crawl out from under their mound of debt, and eventually secure a solid financial future for both themselves and their kids.

By reclaiming ownership of their spending, eliminating their credit card debt, and repaying the money they borrowed from their retirement accounts, they righted the ship and put themselves back in the driver's seat. Their future used to look grim, but, while they still face some challenges in the short term, they will come out ahead in the end.

The fiscal endgame

Like the Barleycorns, our country finds itself at a crossroads. The overspending looms large over our nation, impacting us in subtle and disruptive ways. Every year that we continue to add to the national debt, we further mortgage our future. Every year that we continue to borrow funds from the IGH bucket, we dampen the ability to pay for the full retirement benefits of millions of Americans that have, over the years, contributed their fair share in payroll taxes to the Social Security fund.

Since Richard Nixon broke the seal on the Gold Standard in 1971, on average, every White House administration has submitted a budget of ~20% of the GDP. Since then, we have also spent consistently at a ~25% clip, so it should not surprise anyone that we have accumulated annual ~5% deficits. In 2015, inclusive of the public and IGH portions, the debt ballooned past the GDP of the US and in 2017, we will cross the $20 trillion threshold.

Subsequently, the annual interest payments on the borrowed funds have increased accordingly, currently sitting at nearly a quarter of a trillion dollars. Let that numbing number sink in for a minute. *The annual interest payment has already grown larger than the combined budgets for Education, the Environment, Space & Technology, Agriculture, and Energy.* At the current burn rate, we will reach a $1 trillion debt interest payment in the next decade, and that assumes that the economy does not tank and that the interest rates remain relatively under control.

So, what is the solution for the constant federal overspending? While a balanced budget amendment makes sense, it needs to meet the needs of our country in the 21st century. A Machiavellian "no more overspending" balanced budget amendment would not work in down years or, especially, if the economy fell into an extended funk. The Federal Reserve needs debt in the system, to exercise their Open Market Operations and Discount Rate tools, and to effectively manipulate the direction of the economy. In fact, Congress approving debt instruments so that the public can invest in America by buying US Savings Bonds, has always been an integral part of that equation. For the Barleycorns, a mortgage presents much the same opportunity at the individual level. Jonathan and Maria invested in a home mortgage to gain tax breaks, build up their credit and grow their real estate portfolio. It is the same principle at the federal level; a little debt is not only OK, but it is also necessary. However, how much debt do we need?

Ignoring wars, when we have maintained a ~2% overspend limit, over time the surplus years have balanced out the deficit years. From 1790 to the Civil War, the debt did not increase. From the Civil War to the First World War, the same phenomena occurred. Between WWI and WWII, the roaring 1920s nearly balanced The Great Depression of the 1930s. The time after WWII and into the 1960s remains as the last sustained period where we owned significant surpluses that offset most of the growing deficits. Then the bottom fell out in the 1970s with the elimination of the Gold Standard, the last straw signaling the beginning of the ~5% overspend era. *A 2% cap on the annual deficits seems like a reasonable starting point for a hard debt ceiling as part of a pseudo-balanced budget amendment.*

Just like FDR redefined the social, healthcare and welfare needs of the nation in his time, we need for the leaders in DC to recognize the risks of the continued pattern of overspending and the damage that it spells for future generations. We have so many urgent needs:

- We need to stop compromising the safety net of millions of Social Security recipients

- We need to invest more in education, technology, and the environment to meet the future needs of our children and grandchildren

- We need to add more jobs with higher paying salaries for our workforce

- We need to revamp the aging infrastructure across our nation

- We need to strengthen Homeland Security and our military to increase our safety domestically and abroad

- We need to take better care of our veterans

- We need to develop clean energy sources to undo the damage we have caused the environment

The list goes on ad infinitum. However, we cannot accomplish any of it if we continue to misappropriate billions of dollars on misguided, wasteful spending orchestrated by special interest groups while burning boatloads of cash on senseless debt interest payments.

To succeed, we need to upset the status quo. Similar to Jonathan and Maria, it starts with a serious conversation about the state of affairs, recognizing the unsustainability of the current level of overspending. Next, comes determining the national priorities that will influence the budget. We could engage in an endless debate on the size of the budget, but historically we have yet to retreat on its size relative to the GDP. For this reason, we propose to maintain the spend at the current level of ~25% but refocus wasteful spending into higher priority areas. Let's stop publishing 20% budgets and revenue plans when we know that we will continue to spend 25%. Then comes the hard part. "Right-sizing" the budget to 25% will require a corresponding rise in tax revenues to the level of the new budget.

Like the Barleycorns, we will need to implement an 8-step economic strategy that will be painful at first, but will deliver long-term, lasting prosperity to our nation:

1. Scrutinize – start by scrubbing every budgeted dollar. Referring to the Barleycorn analogy, do not spend $500 a month on a car payment when a $300 vehicle can suffice. Every single one of the over 4,000 line items in the current budget needs to justify their existence and level of

funding, regardless of expenses earmarked mandatory or discretionary.

2. Right-Size the Budget – stop budgeting for 20% when we spend 25%. We need to raise the budget to reflect the needs of 2016 America.

3. Prioritize Spending – we need to invest in America's future. For example, Education, Technology, and the Environment need to rise in the current scheme of national priorities.

4. Raise Revenue – this one is tricky. Skye will tell you to quit pussyfooting and make the top tiers of individuals but, especially, corporations pay their fair share of income taxes. That the behemoths need to contribute to the bottom line, not just in employing Americans but also in tax revenue. Tanner, however, would vehemently voice the opposite view. A supply-sider, he prefers the trickle-down approach of lowering taxes to incentivize consumption and investment.

5. Control – pass a pseudo-Balanced Budget Amendment based on 25% of the GDP.

6. Set a Hard Debt Ceiling – set a 2% hard debt ceiling that accommodates for unplanned emergencies. The debt ceiling needs to carry the weight of a stop sign, not a rolling yield.

7. Stop Borrowing from IGH – quit taking money from other governmental agencies, especially Social Security.

8. Eliminate outstanding commitments – prepare a 20-year plan to pay down the national debt to 2% of the GDP – a level that still affords the Fed enough leeway to maneuver the economy. However, let's start by repaying the funds borrowed from Social Security and IGH.

In summary, while we love to complicate the federal budget, like the Barleycorns, the solution is simple, really. We must eliminate wasteful spending and raise revenues. The looming question in DC, where special interest and lobbyist reign supreme, remains – who will tackle this? The answer is everyone. *This matter is far from a partisan issue, and it will take a concerted effort from both sides of the aisle in the White House and Congress to attack this problem from all angles*. In many ways, the growing national debt stands as much a threat to the future of America as terrorism or global warming.

We need a new plan, a New Deal if you will. This time around we need to fight not for social responsibility and economic reform through governmental oversight. This time around, we need a pledge for fiscal responsibility from Washington. We need to invest in America's future by putting a stop to wasteful spending that starts with getting the debt under control. By taking Washington back, we can then focus the budget on the high value-add programs that will strengthen America and assure our future for generations to come. We would place more emphasis, not only on the mandatory spending earmarked to healthcare, pensions, defense, and welfare, but we would also funnel more money to education, the environment, veteran benefits, and technology, etc. – areas that must take priority and receive the funding required to the long-term success and prosperity of future Americans.

Tanner and Skye

Now let's circle back to the claims on the memes from Tanner and Skye and assess, once and for all, right from left, true right from true wrong. In the first meme from Tanner, he claimed that B. Obama had doubled the debt, stolen more than $2 trillion from Social Security and placed 100+ million recipients on welfare.

His first claim ranks as mathematically correct, similar to the claim that the gun related death rate had increased by 25% in Australia from 2008-2011. The debt rose from $10.0 trillion when B. Obama took office in 2009, to an estimated $19.4 trillion in 2016. However, we can also make a similar claim about the previous president, George W, who also nearly doubled the debt in his eight years in office, from $5.6 to $10.0 trillion. In reality, the debt has grown at a ~5% clip of the GPD since G. Ford took the reins from a disgraced R. Nixon in the mid-1970s. By the way, Tanner's personal hero, Ronald Reagan, nearly tripled the debt from $909 billion to $2.6 trillion.

At the current spend rate, we are doubling the debt just about every eight years or so. If President Trump gets re-elected, he will have the honor of also having doubled the debt during his administration. Moreover, let's not forget that B. Obama also inherited a horrific financial crisis that ruined his budgets for the first three years of his first term, setting his combined budget back nearly two trillion dollars with the Wall Street Bailout and ensuing relief effort to hammer through the Great Recession.

(ASIDE: History tells us that Trump's initial plan to lower individual and corporate tax rates will jump start the economy in a big way, similar to the R. Reagan to B. Clinton era of the 1980s and 1990s. However, depending on how long it takes for the cuts to trickle-down into the consumption and investment buckets to produce tax revenue, there exists a high probability that he will increase and accelerate the growth of the debt at an even higher clip than the current ~5%. However, before we pass judgment, let's see where this self-anointed genius and former reality show host takes us. Politically, he has altered forever the status quo on how the game is played. Now, let's see what he does with the nation's kitty.)

Tanner's second claim regarding B. Obama stealing more than $2 trillion from SS also rates as almost correct. B. Obama did borrow $2.1 trillion from IGH, of which Social Security accounts for about 60%. However, his predecessor owns the largest chunk of borrowed candy from IGH at $2.3 trillion. If we review the amount borrowed from IGH as a percent of the GDP, B. Obama at 1.6% comes in trailing B. Clinton and Bush Sr, both tied at 1.9%, and well behind the clubhouse leader Bush Jr, at 2.3%. FDR and R. Reagan rank as the only other presidents to reach the 1% milestone in funds borrowed from IGH. In a little-publicized fact, B. Obama became the first president since Lyndon Johnson to put money back into IGH, which he accomplished in three of his 8-years in office.

The final claim of welfare recipients growing past the 100 million mark comes as a direct result of the population growth and how we define welfare beneficiaries. Every president will have more welfare recipients than the previous – that results directly from the growing census. The second part, how we define welfare recipients, can vary the results by a wide margin. The government allows participation in a welfare program when an individual or family in need lacks the means to fend for themselves, in so-called "means-tested programs." These programs have strict requirements, for an individual or family's income and assets to fall below specified thresholds, in order to qualify for benefits. The stark reality is this – when we consider all the federal health care, welfare and pensions programs, nearly half of the US population receives some level of federal help.

The specific and now infamous "109 million Americans on welfare" number originated from a Census Bureau study in 2013 that counted all the "means tested" programs and did not include Social

Security recipients. Add the SS beneficiaries, and the 109 would jump to 153 million people on some welfare program in 2012 or 49% of the 309 million US population at the time. The percent of people on welfare programs has steadily increased since the 1960s as the divide between the classes continued to grow. So, in the overall scheme, yes, the welfare census passed the 100 million mark under B. Obama's watch, but it probably would have done so regardless of who resided in the White House. That said, B. Obama did add 11 million ACA recipients to his total which accelerated the growth of his numbers.

Skye had countered Tanner's first meme with typical market index data: the growth of the stock market, the rise in GDP, the lowering of the deficit by $1.6 trillion dollars and the decrease in percent unemployed.

For her first point, the stock exchange is a very volatile animal so to pick two specific points in time without context can cause huge fluctuations in the metrics, depending on what has transpired in the weeks or months before the chosen dates. For example, before the housing bubble in 2008, George W could have claimed that the Dow had increased from 10,900 to 14,200 since he had taken office in 2001. However, due to circumstances beyond his control and placed in motion before his administration, the Dow suddenly crashed, dropping precipitously to 9,000 by the time he left office. B. Obama benefited from a low starting point, and when the Dow recovered to its normal trend, on paper, it gives the impression that he doubled the Dow, from 9,000 to 18,500. In reality, G.W. and B. Obama would have split the difference and the growth under their watch would have looked very similar. For the most part, the long-term performance of the Dow plots as an exponential series. Therefore, most Commanders in Chief could claim an increase in the stock market, unless they presided over an immediate or extended period of economic insecurity. For example, vilified G.W. had the unfortunate luck of presiding through two dreadful droughts in the wake of the burst dot-com bubble, attacks on 9/11 and then the housing crash in 2008, while FDR survived the extended Great Depression and R. Reagan The Great Inflation.

Skye's GDP claim also rates as true, but B. Obama again had a negligible impact upon this metric. As we covered comprehensively, the GDP grows at an exponential rate. Only four events since the Revolutionary War have caused an extended downturn in the GDP: the War for Independence, the War of 1812, the Civil War and The

Great Depression. Unlike these three military conflicts, wars not fought on domestic soil actually increased the productivity of the nation by converting the country's manufacturing base into building war machines, which explains how WWII finally pulled the country out of The Great Depression blues. In fact, every president since the Civil War, except for H. Hoover and FDR, can stake a claim that the GDP grew over his administration. The US population rates as the only factor that ties directly to the growth of the GDP – mo' people, mo' output, mo' money.

Her third point on the deficit we covered in detail, and for the most part, if we ignore the first three years in B. Obama's first term, which included the Wall Street Bailout, his deficits looked very similar to his predecessors going all the way back to R. Reagan. Skye of course, cherry-picked the worst and best deficit years for her analysis to make her guy look good. However, let's give some credit to Barack for recovering the status quo after the economic mess he inherited.

On the jobs claim from Skye, how we measure the unemployment metric has changed over time to make the numbers of the administration du jour look better. B. Obama inherited a rate near ~10% from the Great Recession and had done an admirable job lowering the metric to less than 5%. However, the White House only reports the official U3 unemployment metric. A more comprehensive metric, the U6, includes the discouraged workers and marginally attached, as well as those underemployed working part-time because they cannot find full-time jobs or jobs that do not take full advantage of their capabilities. When we include those ~8 million persons, the actual U6 metric jumps to almost 10%, or twice the value of the U3. To add to the frustration of the unemployed, the type of jobs available have changed dramatically. Since the vast migration of manufacturing jobs overseas, mostly to Asia and Central America starting in the late 1990's, the income level of the types of jobs available have decreased, which ties into the growing gap between the haves and have-nots. So, while there is merit to Skye's claim on B. Obama lowering the U3 unemployment rate, much work remains on this front to reduce the more meaningful U6 rate.

The second meme from Tanner calls attention to wasteful spending in the form of "for life" salaries of senior members of the White House and Congress. This meme is pure garbage. The POTUS is the only federal employee that can claim a salary, in addition to a Secret Service detail for the rest of his life. No one else receives neither wages, healthcare nor pensions for life. They all participate in the regular federal pension program, which like many private pensions, depends on time served and individual contributions. Furthermore, if we were to accumulate the entire salaries of the White House and Congress and the Supreme Court, the total nut would account for a minuscule 0.01% of the budget. So, Tanner, please, quit passing on asinine misinformation from false news blogs.

Skye's counter on wasteful spending, however, is true. There exist numerous watchdog agencies that point out wasteful spending in Washington. However, similar to the supposed cumulative lifetime salaries from Tanner's false meme, the total amount of the savings indicated by Skye's meme also accounted for a tiny percentage of the federal budget. But, hey, we must start somewhere. Just because the amount is relatively small, it does not mean that we should allow its wasteful spending.

The bottom line on the memes for both sides is that they are filled with half-truths and misinformation designed to push their particular biased agenda. Tanner and Skye will probably never see eye to eye. However, while their ideologies sit at magnetic opposites, they can at least agree on the facts. If they each would settle to a mustard seed of open-mindedness with respect to the data, they might just learn to respect each other's point of view, even if just a bit. They could start by meeting on the common ground that after all was said and done, once we parsed and analyzed all the data, there was little difference in budgets and spending from Democrats and Republicans. Over time, for every Yin, there's a Yang balancing the scales of political justice. For every Franklyn Roosevelt, there's a Ronald Reagan. For every Richard Nixon, there's a Bill Clinton. For every George W. Bush, there's a Barack Obama, for every John Kennedy, there's George H.W. Bush. And for every Gerald Ford, there's a Jimmy Carter. In the end, factors outside the normal scope of presidential control, drive spending in ways that most of the time ring predetermined.

However, from the look of things, Skye will have plenty of fodder for the next 4-years with Donald Trump in office. Since election night, she has pushed for a recount, then vehemently supported an amendment to abolish the electoral college (since Hillary Clinton won the popular vote by more than two million ballots), then finally hoped that 37 electors would defect from Trump's camp to deprive him of the Electoral College majority he needed to become president. After passing through the five stages of grief, Skye finally accepted the outcome – that President Elect Donald Trump would take office on January 20, 2017, to officially become the 45th POTUS. However, the battle is not over. She will renew and reenergize her ongoing fight by attending the "Million Women March" in DC come inauguration time.

Meanwhile, Tanner has been uncharacteristically quiet since the election. Less a few "told you so" posts on the reasons behind the gigantic upset pulled off by The Donald, we have barely heard a peep from him. We can only assume that he has probably been too busy gloating nonstop since Nov 8th to engage those he has branded as haters and nay-sayers.

The Trump appointment of Scott Pruitt, to lead the Environmental Protection Agency, generated strong opposition from environmental scholars and, of course, was passionately criticized by Skye. Even the New York Times got into the act describing Pruitt as a climate change denier (Davenport and Liptondec, 2016). On the other hand, Tanner, expectedly, supported the appointment, pointing to the disagreement amongst scientist on the influence of humans on global warming (Idso Carter and Singer, 2015). He also supported Trump's push to unleash America's $50 trillion in untapped shale, oil, and natural gas reserves and the jobs that will create.

In the next installment of Memes and Memes of Misinformation, we will pick up this thread and present the science and facts behind the highly controversial subject of climate change.

To be continued…

Appendix A

List of references

Austin, D Andrew (2015, Oct 1). The Debt Limit: History and Recent Increases. *Congressional Research Service*. Retrieved from https://fas.org/sgp/crs/misc/RL31967.pdf

Bechtel, Brendan (2015, November 27). Emergency, emergency, this is America's infrastructure calling. *USA Today*. Retrieved from http://www.usatoday.com/story/opinion/2015/11/26/infrastructure-spending-building-bechtel-column/76267138/

Benen, Steve (2015, Oct 15). Deficit shrinks by $1 trillion in Obama era. *MSNBC*. Retrieved from http://www.msnbc.com/rachel-maddow-show/deficit-shrinks-1-trillion-obama-era

Board of Governors of the Federal Reserve System. *Financial Accounts of the United States - Z.1*. Retrieved from https://www.federalreserve.gov/releases/z1/current/

Board of Governors of the Federal Reserve System. *Mission*. Retrieved from https://www.federalreserve.gov/aboutthefed/mission.htm

Bregger, John E (1984). The Current Population Survey: A Historical Perspective and BLS' Role. *Bureau of Labor Statistics*. Retrieved from https://www.bls.gov/opub/mlr/1984/06/art2full.pdf

Bregger, John E; Haugen, Steven E. (1995). BLS Introduces New Range of Alternative Unemployment Measures. *Bureau of Labor Statistics*. Retrieved from https://www.bls.gov/opub/mlr/1995/10/art3full.pdf

Bureau of Labor Statistics, US Department of Labor. *Labor Force Statistics from the Current Population Survey*. Retrieved from https://www.bls.gov/cps/cpsaat01.htm

Central Intelligence Agency. *The World Factbook, Country Comparison: Public Debt*. Retrieved from https://www.cia.gov/library/publications/the-world-factbook/rankorder/2186rank.html

Congressional Budget Office. *CBO's 2014 Long-Term Projections for Social Security: Additional Information*. Retrieved from https://www.cbo.gov/publication/49795

Congressional Budget Office. *Budget and Economic Data*. Retrieved from https://www.cbo.gov/about/products/budget-economic-data

Congressional Budget Office. *Trends in Family Wealth, 1989 to 2013*. Retrieved from https://www.cbo.gov/publication/51846

Desilver, Drew (2016, June 20). More older Americans are working, and working more, than they used to. *Pew Research Center*. Retrieved from http://www.pewresearch.org/fact-tank/2016/06/20/more-older-americans-are-working-and-working-more-than-they-used-to/

Hazlitt, Henry. *Economics in One Lesson* (Third Edition). Harper & Bros.: New York & London, 1946. Print.

Higgins, Alan (2013, March 27). Could the Government confiscate your gold? *The Telegraph.* Retrieved from http://www.telegraph.co.uk/finance/personalfinance/investing/gold/9957508/Could-the-Government-confiscate-your-gold.html

Idso, Craig; Carter, Robert M.; and Singer, S. Fred (2015, November 23). Why scientist disagree about global warming. *The Heartland Institute.* Retrieved from https://www.heartland.org/publications-resources/publications/why-scientists-disagree-about-global-warming

International Firearm Injury Prevention and Policy. *Gun Related Deaths in Australia.* Retrieved from www.gunpolicy.org

Internal Revenue Service. *SOI Tax Stats - Corporation Tax Statistics.* Retrieved from https://www.irs.gov/uac/soi-tax-stats-corporation-tax-statistics

Internal Revenue Service. *SOI Tax Stats - Individual Income Tax Return (Form 1040) Statistics.* Retrieved from https://www.irs.gov/uac/soi-tax-stats-individual-income-tax-return-form-1040-statistics

Kleiber, Dr. Christian (2007, January). The Lorenz curve in economics and econometrics. *A publication of the Center of Business and Economics (WWZ), University of Basel.* Retrieved from https://wwz.unibas.ch/uploads/tx_x4epublication/09_07.pdf

Lamb, Evelyn (2012, November 12). Ask Gini: How to Measure Inequality. *Scientific American.* Retrieved from https://www.scientificamerican.com/article/ask-gini/

Roff, Peter (2013, May 28). Who's Checking the Fact Checkers? *US News & World Report.* Retrieved from http://www.usnews.com/opinion/blogs/peter-roff/2013/05/28/study-finds-fact-checkers-biased-against-republicans

Smith, Robert (2011, April 15). When the U.S. Paid Off the Entire National Debt (And Why It Didn't Last). *Planet Money – The World Explained, NPR.* Retrieved from http://www.npr.org/sections/money/2011/04/15/135423586/when-the-u-s-paid-off-the-entire-national-debt-and-why-it-didnt-last

Social Security Administration. *Social Security Trust Fund Data.* Retrieved from https://www.ssa.gov/oact/ProgData/funds.html

Social Security Administration. *Social Security Beneficiary Statistics.* Retrieved from https://www.ssa.gov/oact/STATS/OASDIbenies.html

Steiner, Craig (2011, Aug 22). The Clinton Surplus Myth. *Town Hall Finance.* Retrieved from http://finance.townhall.com/columnists/craigsteiner/2011/08/22/the_clinton_surplus_myth

Sullivan, Meg (2004, August 10). FDR's policies prolonged Depression by 7 years, UCLA economists calculate. *UCLA Newsroom.* Retrieved from http://newsroom.ucla.edu/releases/FDR-s-Policies-Prolonged-Depression-5409

Sullivan, Meg (2009, August 28). Hoover's pro-labor stance helped cause Great Depression, UCLA economist says. *UCLA Newsroom.* Retrieved from http://newsroom.ucla.edu/releases/pandering-to-labor-caused-great-91447

Tax Foundation. *U.S. Federal Individual Income Tax Rates History, 1862-2013 (Nominal and Inflation-Adjusted Brackets).* Retrieved from http://taxfoundation.org/article/us-federal-individual-income-tax-rates-history-1913-2013-nominal-and-inflation-adjusted-brackets

The Laffer Center. *The Laffer Curve.* Retrieved from http://www.laffercenter.com/the-laffer-center-2/the-laffer-curve/

The World Bank. *Gross Domestic Product Ranking Table.* Retrieved from http://data.worldbank.org/data-catalog/GDP

Titcomb, James (2015, Jan 7). How the Bank of England Abandoned the Gold Standard. *The Telegraph.* Retrieved from http://www.telegraph.co.uk/finance/commodities/11330611/How-the-Bank-of-England-abandoned-the-gold-standard.html

Treasury Direct. *Historical Debt Outstanding – Annual.* Retrieved from https://www.treasurydirect.gov/govt/reports/pd/histdebt/histdebt.htm

US Census Bureau. Survey of Income and Program Participation, 1996 and 2008 Panels. *Data.* Retrieved from https://www.census.gov/programs-surveys/sipp/data.html

US Department of the Treasury. *Debt Limit.* Retrieved from https://www.treasury.gov/initiatives/Pages/debtlimit.aspx

US Department of the Treasury. *National Debt.* Retrieved from https://www.treasury.gov/resource-center/faqs/Markets/Pages/national-debt.aspx

Wang, Amy B. (2016, November 16). 'Post-truth' named 2016 word of the year by Oxford Dictionaries. *The Washington Post.* Retrieved from https://www.washingtonpost.com/news/the-fix/wp/2016/11/16/post-truth-named-2016-word-of-the-year-by-oxford-dictionaries/?utm_term=.dbf432fd8c04

White House Office of Management and Budget. *Historical Tables.* Retrieved from https://www.whitehouse.gov/omb/budget/Historicals

Williamson, Samuel H. Daily Closing Values of the DJA in the United States, 1885 to Present. *Measuring Worth, 2016.* Retrieved from https://www.measuringworth.com/datasets/index.php

Appendix B

Presidents of the United States

President	No	Political Party	Deficit (2015 USD)	Annual Deficit (2015 USD)	Federal Budget as % GDP	Federal Spending as % GDP	Over-spend as % GDP	Over-spend as % Budget
George Washington	1	Nonpartisan	$ (0.2)	$ (0.0)	3.2%	3.8%	0.5%	16.7%
John Adams	2	Federalist	$ -	$ -	2.3%	2.3%	0.0%	0.0%
Thomas Jefferson	3	Democratic-Republican	$ 0.6	$ 0.1	1.8%	1.1%	-0.7%	-37.3%
James Madison	4	Democratic-Republican	$ (0.8)	$ (0.1)	2.6%	3.3%	0.7%	26.7%
James Monroe	5	Democratic-Republican	$ 0.7	$ 0.1	2.7%	2.2%	-0.5%	-18.3%
John Quincy Adams	6	Democratic-Republican	$ 0.8	$ 0.2	2.3%	1.4%	-0.9%	-37.5%
Andrew Jackson	7	Democratic	$ 1.8	$ 0.2	1.9%	1.2%	-0.8%	-39.7%
Martin Van Buren	8	Democratic	$ (0.5)	$ (0.1)	2.2%	2.5%	0.3%	14.2%
William Harrison	9	Whig	$ -	$ -	1.8%	1.8%	0.0%	0.0%
John Tyler	10	Whig-Nonpartisan	$ (0.5)	$ (0.2)	1.6%	2.0%	0.4%	25.4%
James Polk	11	Democratic	$ (0.4)	$ (0.1)	1.9%	2.1%	0.2%	10.7%
Zachary Taylor	12	Whig	$ (0.2)	$ (0.2)	2.1%	2.5%	0.4%	20.0%
Millard Fillmore	13	Whig	$ (0.2)	$ (0.1)	1.7%	1.8%	0.1%	7.2%
Franklin Pierce	14	Democratic	$ 0.4	$ 0.1	1.9%	1.7%	-0.1%	-7.4%
James Buchanan	15	Democratic	$ (0.2)	$ (0.1)	1.9%	2.0%	0.1%	3.2%
Abraham Lincoln	16	Republican	$ (27.1)	$ (6.8)	7.4%	13.4%	6.0%	80.7%
Andrew Johnson	17	Democratic	$ (9.6)	$ (2.4)	7.1%	9.1%	2.0%	27.3%
Ulysses Grant	18	Republican	$ 8.0	$ 1.0	3.9%	3.2%	-0.7%	-16.9%
Rutherford Hayes	19	Republican	$ 1.0	$ 0.3	3.1%	3.0%	-0.1%	-4.1%
James Garfield	20	Republican	$ 1.1	$ 1.1	2.6%	2.1%	-0.4%	-16.7%
Chester Arthur	21	Republican	$ 5.3	$ 1.8	2.5%	1.8%	-0.6%	-26.4%
Grover Cleveland	22	Democratic	$ (0.8)	$ (0.1)	2.7%	2.7%	0.0%	1.0%
Benjamin Harrison	23	Republican	$ 2.5	$ 0.6	2.6%	2.4%	-0.2%	-6.3%
William McKinley	25	Republican	$ (9.4)	$ (2.3)	3.1%	3.6%	0.5%	16.1%
Theodore Roosevelt	26	Republican	$ (9.9)	$ (1.2)	2.4%	2.6%	0.2%	8.9%
William Taft	27	Republican	$ (4.5)	$ (1.1)	2.5%	2.7%	0.2%	6.9%
Woodrow Wilson	28	Democratic	$ (253.1)	$ (31.6)	8.2%	12.4%	4.2%	51.1%
Warren Harding	29	Republican	$ 51.7	$ 12.9	5.1%	3.7%	-1.4%	-28.1%
Calvin Coolidge	30	Republican	$ 40.6	$ 10.2	3.7%	2.8%	-1.0%	-25.5%
Herbert Hoover	31	Republican	$ (30.9)	$ (7.7)	5.0%	5.7%	0.8%	15.2%
Franklin Roosevelt	32	Democratic	$ (2,752.3)	$ (211.7)	23.5%	37.3%	13.9%	59.2%
Harry Truman	33	Democratic	$ 1.6	$ 0.2	17.3%	17.3%	0.0%	-0.1%
Dwight Eisenhower	34	Republican	$ (211.9)	$ (26.5)	18.1%	19.0%	0.9%	4.7%
John Kennedy	35	Democratic	$ (121.3)	$ (40.4)	17.9%	19.0%	1.1%	6.1%
Lyndon Johnson	36	Democratic	$ (322.9)	$ (64.6)	17.4%	18.8%	1.4%	8.1%
Richard Nixon	37	Republican	$ (499.0)	$ (83.2)	17.8%	19.3%	1.5%	8.4%
Gerald Ford	38	Republican	$ (492.0)	$ (246.0)	19.7%	23.8%	4.1%	20.5%
Jimmy Carter	39	Democratic	$ (786.3)	$ (196.6)	19.7%	22.6%	2.9%	14.5%
Ronald Reagan	40	Republican	$ (3,279.7)	$ (410.0)	21.3%	26.4%	5.0%	23.6%
George HW Bush	41	Republican	$ (2,262.6)	$ (565.6)	20.9%	26.7%	5.7%	27.4%

Bill Clinton	42	Democratic	$ (2,364.6)	$ (295.6)	18.8%	21.3%	2.5%	13.1%
George W Bush	43	Republican	$ (5,179.3)	$ (647.4)	18.8%	23.1%	4.2%	22.5%
Barack Obama	44	Democratic	$ (9,920.6)	$ (1,240.1)	21.9%	29.2%	7.3%	33.3%

Appendix C

Wars & Major Economic Events

President	Event
James Madison	War of 1812
Abraham Lincoln	Civil War
William McKinley	Spanish-American War
Woodrow Wilson	World War I
Herbert Hoover	The Great Depression
Franklin Roosevelt	The Great Depression & World War II
Harry Truman	World War II
Dwight Eisenhower	Korean War
Lyndon Johnson	Vietnam War
Richard Nixon	Vietnam War
Jimmy Carter	The Great Inflation
George HW Bush	Iraq War I
George W Bush	Afghanistan War & Iraq War II
Barack Obama	Afghan War, Iraq War II, The Great Recession

Appendix D

Intra-Governmental Holdings Trust Funds

1. Federal Old-Age and Survivors Insurance Trust Fund
2. Civil Service Retirement and Disability Fund, Office of Personnel Management
3. Department of Defense, Military Retirement Fund
4. Federal Hospital Insurance Trust Fund
5. Department of Defense, Medicare Eligible Retiree Fund
6. Federal Disability Insurance Trust Fund
7. Federal Supplementary Medical Insurance Trust Fund
8. Nuclear Waste Disposal Fund, Department of Energy
9. Postal Service Retiree Health Benefits Fund
10. Employees' Life Insurance Fund, Office of Personnel Management
11. Deposit Insurance Fund
12. Unemployment Trust Fund
13. Employees' Health Benefits Fund, Office of Personnel Management
14. Exchange Stabilization Fund, Office of the Secretary, Treasury
15. Pension Benefit Guaranty Corporation
16. Foreign Service Retirement and Disability Fund
17. Airport and Airway Trust Fund
18. National Credit Union Share Insurance Fund
19. Harbor Maintenance Trust Fund
20. National Service Life Insurance Fund, Department of Veterans Affairs
21. Overseas Private Investment Corporation, Insurance and Equity Non Credit Account
22. Assets Forfeiture Fund, Justice
23. Uranium Enrichment and Decommissioning Fund, Department of Energy
24. Vaccine Injury Compensation Trust Fund
25. Oil Spill Liability Trust Fund
26. District of Columbia Federal Pension Trust Fund
27. Farm Credit Insurance Fund, Capital Corporation Investment Fund, Farm Credit Administration
28. Hazardous Substance Superfund
29. Postal Service Fund
30. Treasury Forfeiture Fund
31. Abandoned Mines Reclamation Fund, Office of Surface Mining Reclamation and Enforcement
32. Child Enrollment Contingency Fund
33. Highway Trust Fund
34. Aviation Insurance Revolving Fund

35. Veterans Special Life Insurance Fund, Trust Revolving Fund, Department of Veterans Affairs
36. Sport Fish Restoration and Boating Trust Fund
37. Guarantees of Mortgage-Backed Securities Fund, Government National Mortgage, Housing and Urban Development Association
38. Department of Defense, Education Benefits Fund
39. United States Enrichment Corporation Fund
40. Federal Aid to Wildlife Restoration, United States Fish and Wildlife Service
41. Environmental Improvement and Restoration Fund
42. Leaking Underground Storage Tank Trust Fund
43. Assessment Funds, Office of the Comptroller of the Currency
44. Support for US Relocation to Guam Activities
45. Social Security Equivalent Benefit Account, Railroad Retirement Board
46. FSLIC Resolution Fund, The
47. Railroad Retirement Account
48. National Service Trust, Corporation for National and Community Services
49. Southern Nevada Public Land Management Act of 1998
50. Lower Colorado River Basin Development Fund, Bureau of Reclamation
51. Judicial Survivors Annuities Fund
52. Bonneville Power Administration Fund, Power Marketing Administration, Dept. of Energy
53. Natural Resource Damage Assessment and Restoration Fund, US Fish and Wildlife Service, Interior
54. Judicial Officers Retirement Fund
55. Securities and Exchange Commission Investor Protection Fund
56. Temporary Corporate Credit Union Stabilization Fund
57. Patient-Centered Outcomes Research Trust Fund
58. Gulf Coast Restoration Trust Fund
59. Voluntary Separation Incentive Fund, Defense
60. Prison Industries Fund, Department of Justice
61. United States Trustee System Fund, Justice
62. Veterans Reopened Insurance Fund
63. Utah Reclamation Mitigation and Conservation Account, Interior
64. Native American Institutions Endowment Fund
65. District of Columbia Judges Retirement Fund
66. Central Liquidity Facility, National Credit Union Administration
67. South Dakota Terrestrial Wildlife Habitat Restoration Trust Fund
68. Commodity Futures Trading Commission Customer Protection Fund, Commodity Futures Trading Commission
69. General Post Fund, National Homes, Department of Veterans Affairs
70. Federal Housing Finance Board Working Capital Fund

71. Trust Fund, The Barry Goldwater Scholarship and Excellence in Education Fund
72. Armed Forces Retirement Home Trust Fund
73. Financial Research Fund
74. Expenses, Presidio Trust
75. Operating Fund, National Credit Union Administration
76. Harry S Truman Memorial Scholarship Trust Fund, Harry S Truman Scholarship Foundation
77. Panama Canal Commission Compensation Fund
78. Cheyenne River Sioux Tribe Terrestrial Wildlife Habitat Restoration Trust Fund
79. War-Risk Insurance Revolving Fund, Maritime Administration
80. Inland Waterways Trust Fund
81. Lincoln County Land Act
82. Japan-United States Friendship Trust Fund, Japan-United States Friendship Commission
83. Revolving Fund for Administrative Expense, Farm Credit Administration
84. James Madison Memorial Fellowship Foundation Fund
85. Operation and Maintenance, Indian Irrigation Systems, Bureau of Indian Affairs
86. Court of Veterans Appeals Retirement Fund
87. Claims Court Judges Retirement Fund
88. Morris K Udall Scholarship and Excellence in National Environmental Policy Trust Fund
89. National Institutes of Health Unconditional Gift Fund
90. Tennessee Valley Authority Fund
91. Energy Employees Occupational Illness Compensation Fund
92. Power Systems, Indian Irrigation Projects, Bureau of Indian Affairs
93. Host Nation Support for US Relocation Activities Account
94. Lower Brule Sioux Tribe Terrestrial Wildlife Habitat Restoration Trust Fund
95. Conditional Gift Fund, General, Department of State
96. International Center for Middle Eastern-Western Dialogue Trust Fund
97. John C Stennis Center for Public Service Training and Development
98. Science, Space and Technology Education Trust Fund, National Aeronautics and Space Administration
99. Library of Congress Gift Fund
100. Library of Congress Trust Fund
101. National Archives Trust Fund, National Archives and Records Administration
102. Capitol Visitor Center Revolving Fund
103. Community Development Credit Union Revolving Fund National Credit Union Administration
104. Tax Court Judges Survivors Annuity Fund

105. Capitol Preservation Fund, US Capitol Preservation Commission
106. United States Government Life Insurance Fund, Department of Veterans Affairs
107. Defense Cooperation Account, Defense
108. Eisenhower Exchange Fellowship Program Trust Fund
109. Department of Defense General Gift Fund, Defense
110. United States Naval Academy General Gift Fund
111. Open World Leadership Center Trust Fund
112. Israeli Arab Scholarship Program, United States Information Agency
113. National Security Education Trust Fund
114. Department of the Army General Gift Fund
115. FHA General and Special Risk Insurance Fund, Liquidating Account, Housing and Urban Development
116. National Gift Fund, National Archives and Records Administration
117. Public Health Service Conditional Gift Fund, Health Resources and Services Administration
118. Department of the Navy General Gift Fund
119. Retired Employees' Health Benefits Fund, Office of Personnel Management
120. Coast Guard General Gift Fund
121. Department of the Air Force General Gift Fund
122. Gifts and Bequests, Treasury
123. Gifts and Donations, National Endowment of the Arts
124. Servicemen's Group Life Insurance Fund
125. Endeavor Teacher Fellowship Trust Fund
126. Esther Cattell Schmitt Gift Fund, Treasury
127. National Institutes of Health Conditional Gift Fund
128. Oliver Wendell Holmes Devise Fund, Library of Congress
129. Patients Benefit Fund, National Institutes of Health
130. Preservation, Birthplace of Abraham Lincoln, National Park Service
131. Senate Preservation Trust Fund

Appendix E

FDR Alphabet Soup New Deal Agencies

Alphabet Agency	Year Founded	Name of Agency
AAA	1933	Agricultural Adjustment Administration
CWA	1933	Civil Works Administration
CCC	1933	Civilian Conservation Corps
DRS	1935	Drought Relief Service
EBA	1933	Emergency Banking Act
FLSA	1938	Fair Labor Standards Act
FCA	1933	Farm Credit Administration
FSA	1935	Farm Security Administration
FAP	1935	Federal Art Project (part of WPA)
FAA	1933	Federal Aviation Administration
FCC	1934	Federal Communications Commission
FDIC	1933	Federal Deposit Insurance Corporation
FERA	1933	Federal Emergency Relief Administration
FHA	1934	Federal Housing Administration
FMP	1935	Federal Music Project (part of WPA)
FSRC	1933	Federal Surplus Relief Corporation
FTP	1935	Federal Theatre Project (part of WPA)
FWA	1939	Federal Works Agency
FWP	1935	Federal Writers' Project (part of WPA)
HOLC	1933	Home Owners' Loan Corporation
NIRA	1933	National Industrial Recovery Act
NLRA	1935	National Labor Relations Act
NLRB	1934	National Labor Relations Board/The Wagner Act
NRA	1933	National Recovery Administration
NYA	1935	National Youth Administration
PWA	1933	Public Works Administration
PRRA	1933	Puerto Rico Reconstruction Administration
RA	1935	Resettlement Administration
REA	1935	Rural Electrification Administration (now Rural Utilities Service)
SEC	1934	Securities and Exchange Commission
SSA	1935	Social Security Administration
SSB	1935	Social Security Board (now Social Security Administration)
DSH	1933	Subsistence Homesteads Division
TVA	1933	Tennessee Valley Authority
USHA	1937	United States Housing Authority
USMC	1936	United States Maritime Commission
WPA	1935	Works Progress Administration

Biography

Julio C Castañeda Jr emigrated from Cuba to the US in 1974, grew up in South Florida and currently resides in California with his wife and youngest son. He graduated from Georgia Tech with a Master of Science in Mechanical Engineering and has worked for Motorola, Google and Snap Inc. for more than 25 years in product development, R&D, and manufacturing. Over the course of his career, Julio has earned a Master Six Sigma Black Belt, been granted 48 US patents and authored numerous technical reports on a broad range of engineering topics. An avid sports fan and fascinated by the statistical aspect of sports, he has published two books in a series titled "Football Morsels" redefining quarterback and team statistics. In this book, the first installment of the "Misinformation" series, Julio uses his statistical approach and data based conclusions to provide a balanced and unbiased presentation of key socioeconomic and political issues.

Preview

In the next "Misinformation" installment, we will take a stab at presenting both sides of a highly controversial subject – global warming. In the face of overwhelming data that unequivocally points to a trend of rising temperatures and carbon dioxide, how can the two sides of this argument draw opposite conclusions from the same data set? Alternatively, perhaps the argument lays not so much on the whether the mean temperature of the planet continues to rise, but on what has caused the increase. One side, the treehugging Chicken Little camp led by Skye, vehemently blames the human race's neverending thirst for dirty sources of energy. Meanwhile, the other side, Tanner and his petroleum-loving cowboys, shrug their shoulders claiming that the earth's cyclic patterns are just rearing their ugly heads once again while driving their Humvees with "Don't worry, be happy" bumper stickers. After all, let's not forget that just a few decades ago, environmentalists proclaimed that Planet Earth was headed into an inevitable deep freeze. We will present some of the key metrics of this very complex argument for both sides, and when done we will draw some conclusions of our own.

Index